Because the Horn
Is There

D0048019

Other Sailing Classics

MILES SMEETON

Because the Horn
Is There

*Mallory, shortly before his last attempt
to climb Mount Everest, when he was lost
with his companion Irvine high near the
summit, was asked what drove him to
attempt it.*

'Because it is there,' he replied.

GRAFTON BOOKS

A Division of the Collins Publishing Group

LONDON GLASGOW
TORONTO SYDNEY AUCKLAND

Grafton Books
A Division of the Collins Publishing Group
8 Grafton Street, London W1X 3LA

First published in Great Britain by Nautical Publishing Co. 1970
Reissued by Granada Publishing 1985
Reprinted by Grafton Books 1987

Copyright © 1970 Gray's Publishing Ltd

British Library Cataloguing in Publication Data

Smeeton, Miles
    Because the Horn is there.
    1. Voyages and travels – 1951-
    2. Yachts and yachting
    I. Title
    910.4'5   G540
ISBN 0–246–12672–8

Printed in Great Britain by
Billing & Sons Ltd., Worcester

All rights reserved. No part of this publication may be
reproduced, stored in a retrieval system or transmitted,
in any form or by any means, electronic, mechanical,
photocopying, recording or otherwise, without the prior
permission of the publisher.

Contents

Thanks are due to *Blackwood's Magazine* for permission to quote from the experiences of a visitor to Porto Praia in 1806.

To BILL TILMAN, soldier, mountaineer, sailor, and torchbearer, and his ship, *Mischief*.

Que es mi barco — mi tesoro.
Que es mi Dios — la libertad.
Mi ley la fuerza y el viento.
Mi unica patria la mar.

CHAPTER ONE

Yarmouth

When the shadows forsook the cliffs under which we were anchored, *Tzu Hang*, with a long grumble from her anchor chain, told us that the tide had changed. We hove up the anchor and motored close round the red and white lighthouse and the steep grey rocks of the Needles, which had only just emerged from summer fog. The fog was breaking up into scattered cloud through which the sun shone. Ahead and to port a long, low sandy headland appeared, to starboard the green fields and woodlands of the Isle of Wight, and the sun-dappled water in between was spotted with yacht sails.

We had only seen the Needles once before, at the start of a passage to Spain which had turned into an almost unplanned voyage round the world in an easterly direction. A voyage that had taken us and the Siamese cat, Pwe, as far south as Durban and as far north as the Bering Sea and had been completed the previous autumn at the green, enclosed harbour of Kinsale in Eire, where *Tzu Hang* had spent the winter on a mooring, close below cows and gorse and a ruined castle. Now we were about to end our easterly progress before we reversed our navigational trend, and since the distance to Yarmouth was so short and the wind so light we kept the motor running, feeling a little guilty as we passed yachts that were sailing, a little relieved when a burble from their exhausts proclaimed that they were motoring too.

As we rounded the buoy outside Yarmouth breakwater, wondering where we should go and what sort of welcome we should meet with, or what confusion and consternation we might cause, the masts of the yachts inside showed like a bivouac of lancers, or the field of some mediaeval tournament. Here were Sir Lancelots and Percevals, Don Quixotes and Sancho Panzas, here were great hopes and sad disappointments, and here now came one errant knight, in battered red surcoat, full of strange but hopefully modest stories of far countries and foreign waters.

The doubts with which we approached this 'caravanserai', this sanctuary of British yachtsmen, were put to rest as we entered the harbour. We were met by the Harbourmaster, rowing a dinghy stern foremost in the fairway. He wore a fisherman's jersey and a white-topped peaked cap. His weather-beaten face shone with welcome and enjoyment and his voice rang across the water with assurance and vast authority. No matter what wealth or position, what experience or inexperience be yours, here was a voice to be smartly obeyed.

'Here you are,' he called, suddenly switching to rowing ahead, 'turn her up here. Now follow me. Where are you from? Tie up alongside that big motor cruiser. They'll take your lines. Got to go now. Another yacht coming in.' He switched again to astern and went off to meet it. On week-ends he must have rowed 50 miles at least. He moved like a water-beetle in a duck pond and the harbour board should have given him a double ender. He was known to everyone as Charlie. The very essence of the British stock that has founded the English speaking countries of the world, he was cheerful, incorruptible, hardworking, finding fulfilment in an idea of service, and if he read this he'd say—'For Christ's sake'.

When a ship has cruised as much as *Tzu Hang* she will meet in almost any port a friend whom she has met somewhere else in the world. We had barely tied up before we saw Geoffrey Pearce and his wife, Elisabeth, rowing out to *Tzu Hang* in a dinghy as broad-beamed and unsinkable as Geoffrey himself. We had met them first in Singapore when he was in charge of the Dockyard. There they had made us at home in their lovely house with its huge rooms and wide verandahs and Geoffrey had arranged for various repairs that *Tzu Hang* required. Now he was recently retired from the Navy, and was finding a house in Freshwater barely large enough to contain his many interests, signs of which were stacked in every room. As before, they gave us the use of their house and a car, and we were soon tied up alongside *Ulva*, his big motor sailer. *Ulva* had two brass-bound heads of noble proportions and smooth efficiency, and various bunks and staterooms, so that half *Tzu Hang*'s crew; my daughter, Clio, and her husband, Alex, and their nine-month-old daughter, could take up temporary residence. They had come across from Eire with us and were soon to leave us for a job in Spain.

Ulva had a long propeller shaft that ran from the engine forward almost the whole length of the ship, supported by numerous bearings that at sea had to be frequently checked and oiled. Most people would have found these bearings a trial, but Geoffrey seemed to regard them with satisfaction. It must have been something about the long shaft, the oil can and the wipey in his hand that reminded him that he was first and last a ship's engineer. Even his house had sprouted a complexity of large copper pipes in a water system that he had installed with wonderful skill, although with some disregard for ceilings, and which no doubt reminded him of the insides of a ship from which indeed they had come.

They took us ashore to dinner and soon had asked the inevitable question, 'Where are you off to next?'

'Well—back to Canada in the autumn,' we replied, and I don't think anyone asked by which way.

This was just as well, because we were planning to go back to the west coast of Canada by way of Cape Horn. Not through the Channels or the Straits of Magellan, but by the old ocean route that had twice beaten us in 1957, only this way we were going to try it in the opposite direction, the most difficult way. We did not want to tell anyone this, because we imagined them saying later, 'Now they are really going round the bend'.

In spite of Sir Francis Chichester's example, the possibilities of adventure get progressively less as one gets older, so that, since we were in England and had to go back to Canada, we might just as well take this opportunity to sail round Cape Horn while we were young enough—or rather not too old—to do it. Since our two attempts in 1957 we had sailed many thousands of miles in high latitudes and stormy oceans. Nowhere had we met anything like the two gales that had nearly brought *Tzu Hang* to disaster. Then we thought that the weather that we had encountered was really natural to an attempt to round Cape Horn. Now we know that both were severe storms; being more experienced and better able to judge wind force and wave height. It is always possible to meet another such storm but unlikely that we should do it three times running, and anyway most unlikely that we should meet the sort of wave that pitchpoled *Tzu Hang*. As for being rolled over, nothing would ever induce me to lie a-hull again in heavy seas.

If *Tzu Hang* was as seaworthy as we believed her to be, then it was high time that we proved it, and her success would underline the unquestionable fact that even an able yacht may be overwhelmed in heavy seas, particularly in high latitudes south and west of Cape Horn, or in winter in the North Atlantic and North Pacific. Let *Tzu Hang* make a successful trip in the most difficult direction and her first failure would no longer be written off by other aspirants, to bad hull design or faulty seamanship, but rather to the luck of the weather to which all ships are liable.

It is easy to write like this in retrospect in justification of a third attempt to round Cape Horn. In fact the reasons were rather simpler and more primitive. The first reason was Beryl. She never likes giving up something that she has started to do, and the fact that we had failed to get *Tzu Hang* round Cape Horn had rankled for years. Her love of adventure smoulders within her like an eternal flame. If a flying saucer landed in front of us and an insect hand beckoned us on board, she would step inside without hesitation, while I, distrustful and suspicious behind the nearest bush, would watch the door close and Beryl take off for infinity. I would have the compensation of knowing that my wife, eyes alight while the spacemen flinched from her gesticulations, was already engaged in some form of conversation, eagerly tasting space food, and enjoying every moment of her voyage.

When she had rejoined me in the spring in Eire, after a visit to see our daughter in South Africa, I suggested that we should return to the east coast of Canada and have a look at Labrador. 'Labrador,' said Beryl, 'why don't we go back to the West Coast of Canada and go there by Cape Horn? Everyone seems to sail round Cape Horn now and I'm sure we can do it. Anyway, I'd like to do it for *Tzu Hang*.'

It was the moment of truth that I had been expecting for years. As far as I was concerned, I thought that *Tzu Hang* had done pretty well down there and was quite prepared to leave it at that and to stick in the northern hemisphere. One can laugh off these wifely suggestions once or twice but finally it gets to a point where a choice must be made. I could swing once more on that rope of youthful enjoyment and adventure that had supported us through 30 years of excitement and vicissitudes, whose strands were wearing a bit thin but which would surely support us a little longer, or I could let go— Beryl never—and slip into the cesspool of increasing infirmity and boring reminiscences. Beryl had me on the spot, and I too felt that *Tzu Hang* would certainly do it on the third try, but it was in our own ability that I had some doubt.

'Not by ourselves,' I said. 'We'll have to get a good man to come with us.'

'Well then, write to Bob Nance,' she said. 'He's just waiting for a chance to go down there again.' Bob was the second and best reason for our third attempt.

We had met him two years before in San Francisco, on Andy Wall's 30-foot Australian sloop, *Carronade*, just about to set off for Tahiti, and from there on a passage round Cape Horn. He was then 26 years old, broad shouldered and narrow waisted, brown from the tropical sun, having recently come up from the South Sea Islands. In most ways he was a typical young Australian, but more reserved and quietly spoken than the average. He had broad feet from going barefoot in his native woods about Wallaby Creek and moved like a cat on deck. His brother,

5

Bill Nance, had recently completed a circumnavigation south of the three great capes, Cape of Good Hope, Cape Leeuwin and Cape Horn, starting from England, in the 25-foot sloop *Cardinal Vertue*. This must be the greatest singlehanded circumnavigation of all time, because it was done without financial backing or the spur of publicity and the distances and times were fantastic. He averaged 123 miles a day from New Zealand to the River Plate, but all his times were comparative.

When Bill arrived in Melbourne and later in New Zealand, Bob had found time off from the bank in which he was working to help his brother refit and prepare for the voyage across the Southern Ocean, and thereafter decided that banking as a way of life was not for him. He determined also to go to sea in small ships, to gain experience until he was ready to build his own yacht and travel his own way. Knowing also from his business experience and from a quiet confidence in his own ability, that he could always make money when he applied himself to that necessary task. He was no slouch in getting experience, for the first yacht that he went on was wrecked on a South Sea Island reef.

We didn't see much of him but saw enough to know that no one could ask for a better companion at sea. He asked if we were looking for someone to come with us to Iceland, and said he'd like to do so after *Carronade* had been round Cape Horn, but *Carronade* found such hospitality in the ports on the south and east coasts of South America, that she had only arrived in Miami that spring. I wrote to him and had an immediate reply. I had mentioned only the Channels, but Bob wrote: 'I think I shall try and persuade you to take her round Cape Horn and not through the Channels. I think you owe it her.' So here was Bob, coming to join us in August, and we all had the same idea.

The last and quite the worst reason for another attempt was that two yachts no better than *Tzu Hang* had recently rounded the Cape and a yachting magazine had published a letter about heavy weather sailing in which, referring to *Tzu Hang*'s attempt, the author had written; '*Tzu Hang*? She was a wrong

6

'un, although she was badly let down by her crew.' The author also claimed to have sailed through the Aleutian Islands, but it must have been after we were there, as no one mentioned his voyage to us. Nor, although he claimed to have made two single-handed passages from New Zealand round Cape Horn and to have spent many months in the Channels, was he known of by the Chileans and Argentinians, who watch each other and their passages and islands so zealously. At least the crew of *Carronade* never heard of him from the naval garrisons of Ushuaia and Puerto Williams, who knew everything about all the other Cape Horn yachtsmen. I did not bother to take up the challenge, but perhaps somewhere deep in my subconscious mind I was mulling over the remark in anger. '*Tzu Hang* a wrong 'un?' *Tzu Hang* who had carried us safely for 100,000 miles round the world and back, up to the Arctic Circle and down to 52°S. We had better show how right she is.

If Yarmouth harbour had reminded me of the field of a mediaeval tournament then the tent of the lord marshal, with the heralds and the judges, was undoubtedly the fuel dock, where there was a small office almost entirely filled by Mrs Lakeman, and a workshop presided over by her husband, Robin. Robin Lakeman was assisted by another engineer known as Arthur. Robin had a deep dislike for outboard engines, of which there were at least 20 under repair in the shop, and held all yachtsmen, at least in regard to their engineering ability, in disdain. He was the most taciturn man, always sucking a pipe and saying nothing, but looking everything. Every yachts man sought, but never won, his approval, and a smile or a dry joke was like the rain that breaks a drought.

Once a week Robin escaped from yachtsmen and took a day off in London. I always wondered what he did. Did he wander elegantly dressed down Bond Street and across St James' Park? Did he suck a pipe behind his paper in some Victorian club room and glower at strangers as he did a suppliant with a faulty outboard? Or did he spend his afternoon watching football at Twickenham or cricket at Lord's? Five pounds to a penny it was the latter.

7

Arthur was rarely seen except upside down, as unless he was at his post of lifeboat mechanic he was always missing in whatever goes for an engine-room in a yacht. This position had given him a long dour face, which rarely lit up except on the discovery of some disaster such as a hole in the cylinder block. Arthur always referred to me, when talking to Beryl, as 'He'. 'He says he wants the head put right. What's wrong with it? I don't like nothing to do with heads. He'd better take it to pieces himself and bring it round to the shop.'

Alex had been blamed for the stoppage of the head in Ireland and had attempted to take it to pieces and put it right. When I had dismantled it again, and shown it to Arthur in the shop, he gave it a brief look:

'Of course everything comes back,' he said. 'It's got no stop-and-go valve.'

'I'm sure its got everything. It used to work perfectly.'

'Not in a thousand years. You go back and look at the diagram and you'll find there's a valve missing. I suppose you've got a diagram?' he said suspiciously.

I had—and found that there was a valve missing, called the 'joker valve'. It turned out that the fastidious Alex with head averted and eyes tight shut had thrown it overboard by mistake. The valve was appropriately named for Arthur's eyes lit up when I confessed, and no doubt he tells the story amongst others when *Tzu Hang*'s name crops up—'and do you know what? He'd lost the ruddy joker valve.'

Unlike the taciturn Robin and the dour Arthur, Mrs Lakeman radiated good humour. She was a big-hearted, vigorous woman, but owing to some accident when she was a girl, had lost an arm. This incapacitated her not at all, for she seemed, like Kali, to have half a dozen; one to tuck the telephone under her chin, one to put a receipt on a hook, one to handle the fuel bowser, one to catch a line, one to wave to a yacht leaving the harbour, and one to poke you a hammer blow in the ribs if you teased her, all of which actions could go on simultaneously.

'It's a shame,' said a visiting American yachtsman. 'They

8

should give you a proper office, not a little cubby hole like this. You should come to America. They'd give you some room and a big desk there.'

'What's wrong with my office? I can only get one man at a time in here and that's how I like it. Nice and cozy.' She gave him a ponderous wink but she never forgave him for the description.

Beryl took all her problems to Mrs Lakeman and for everything she had an answer so that we referred to her as 'The Oracle'. After we had been there a couple of weeks we found that she had been christened 'Delphie'. The Oracle sat in her shrine from early morning until late at night, except for sudden forays to do with yacht arrivals at the fuel dock. Often we came back late at night after dining out to find her there alone, the rain on the window, the radio on, her kettle steaming, her glasses on her nose, a book in her hand, available to dispense wisdom, prophecy or fuel as required.

These three tended to the needs of all the yachts in the yacht harbour and bossed and directed the visitors who arrived. They must have puzzled some of the foreigners but they, like Charlie, were so sturdily English that they might have stepped out of some English film. Hereward the Wake in the Fens surely had a Robin Lakeman at his side, who silently knocked straying Normans on the head, an Arthur who chiselled off the rivets of their armour, and a Delphie who spurred on the men and hid the traces of their deeds in the sedge. It was into these kindly, capable, and critical hands that *Tzu Hang* now fell.

Meanwhile, Bob arrived with a huge roll of charts from *Carronade* and a very small duffle bag, stepping, in almost 24 hours, from the deck of *Carronade* in Miami on to the deck of *Tzu Hang* in Yarmouth, and immediately set about her care. Very soon we began to wonder how on earth we had ever managed without him. We had been unable to get the red vinyl paint with which her topsides had been painted until too late so that she was looking rather tatty amongst the spruce yachts in the harbour. Now we had paint from England and

9

America but as it was getting near our sailing time we decided to leave the topsides until we got a chance to do something in a better climate in Spain. Bob started on the doghouse and hatches which are white, like her rail, boom, and masts, and soon *Tzu Hang*'s appearance began to improve.

We were beginning to wonder whether the engine, which had a leaky water pump and fuel filter, would be ready in time to leave at the end of August, for Arthur remained invisible, but one day he had obviously materialized, for I found all the fuel pipes gone.

'There's nothing wrong with those pipes,' he said, when I found him, 'I couldn't find any stoppage. I've blown through them all.'

'No. It was the filter that was leaking,' I said.

'I was told,' said Arthur, mentioning no names, 'I was told that the fuel lines were plugged.'

'And the water pump is leaking,' I told him.

'Those things always leak,' he said gloomily.

Some days later everything was in place but the engine wouldn't start. Finally Robin, the chief surgeon, was called in. I was away, but Beryl was there.

'We'll have to take the cylinder head off,' said Robin at last, with a suck at his pipe.

'Well, He told me that the Irish had overhauled it completely,' said Arthur. Here Arthur was mistaken, it was the leaky water pump that had been completely overhauled, and leaked as badly as ever.

The cylinder head came off. 'Well for heaven's sake,' said Robin startled out of his taciturnity, 'is that what the Irish did? How does he expect an engine to run in that condition?'

'Well, He said it was going all right, that's what He said,' replied Arthur.

When I got back the engine had dissolved into small pieces but it was finally reassembled in time for us to leave. Since then it has continued to run, as indeed it usually does when required, but the filter and the water pump leaked as much as ever, and it was not until we reached Montevideo, where the Uruguayans, due to import restrictions, are adept at keeping old motors running, that I finally got them fixed.

While we were in Yarmouth we often heard someone say as a yacht went past, 'There's *Tzu Hang*', or 'There's that cat'. Even Eric Tabarly, over from France for a race, spent some time sculling in the channel beside her while he studied her hull, no doubt calculating how she came to be pitchpoled. When the day came to leave we were conscious that we were not absolutely unknown, and therefore were specially anxious not to make any mistakes. It was Bob's first experience of sailing with us, and to ensure that we made a successful navigation of the Lymington River and found the new yacht marina there, I had asked Erroll Bruce, famous ocean racing skipper and publisher, whether he would like to sail across with us. He was to come over from Lymington on the four o'clock ferry.

Soon after lunch we started the engine and drew back out of a sandwich of yachts into the fairway. In order to have some control if the engine stopped, as there was a fresh wind, I kept a bow line to *Ulva* until we were clear. It was fortunate that I did so as the grub screw which secured the shaft to the drive had dropped out and the shaft had become disconnected. We hung ingloriously on to *Ulva* until I could arrange a tow round to the fuel quay. Eventually the grub screw was replaced but not before Beryl had left to do some shopping thinking we would not get away. I rang up Erroll to say that we would not be ready. The rain was pouring down and the wind stirred the yachts at their moorings and I began to think that it was just as well. Erroll would not be put off. 'I'll be over on the six o'clock ferry,' he said, 'you'll surely be ready by then.'

We were, but only just. The engine was running when I saw Beryl loaded with parcels coming up the quay and Erroll in yellow oilskins on the ferry as it docked.

'We're going,' I said, and almost before she had realized the change in plan she was in the cockpit at the helm, with Erroll beside her. Bob and I cast off and we pulled away from the

dock and across the top end of the harbour. As we approached
the point where it was necessary to turn down the far lane
between moored yachts for the harbour entrance, I saw the
tide was running swiftly towards the harbour mouth down the
channel. I walked down the deck and told Beryl that we had a
fast-tide running. It was a mistake. At the corner round which
we were about to turn there was a large ketch moored, with a
long bowsprit projected towards the fairway. Beryl in her
imagination saw herself being carried down until the bowsprit
caught in *Tzu Hung*'s mizzen. Giving it a wide berth she held
on until she was well past before beginning her turn. By now the
tide had got under *Tzu Hang*'s deep keel aft, and she wouldn't
answer readily to the helm.

I saw that we weren't going to clear the yachts on the port
side. 'You'd better check her astern,' I called to Beryl, and
then as her bow began to swing, 'I think you are all right now.'

We were but only by a matter of inches. *Tzu Hang* sidled up
to a much smaller yacht, and then Beryl, trying to edge her
back into the fairway, gave her a fraction too much helm so
that *Tzu Hang*, pivoting slightly, brushed the other yacht with
her side. It was only question of half an inch more and we would
have cleared her. The other yacht bounded sideways in a
manner that I thought was really over-emphasizing such a
gentle kiss and there was a startled shriek from below, as a girl
and a man came tumbling up on deck.

'It's quite all right, there's no damage,' I called cheerily as
we left them craning over the side of their ship.

We couldn't stop and we couldn't very well hide ourselves
in shame, so it seemed that the best thing to do was to go on as
if nothing—or hardly anything—had happened. Fog-horns
and car horns were blowing a farewell to us, but we felt that
they were screaming in ridicule. Bob's eyes opened wide—
perhaps it was the beginning of a disillusionment—and Erroll
was no doubt hoping that he hadn't been recognized. *Tzu
Hang* flew over to Lymington and in two days we were off on
our adventure, but I have often thought of the owners of the
other boat and wished that I had been able to apologize.

When we arrived in Montevideo there was a letter waiting from friends in Yarmouth. 'You certainly left your mark on Yarmouth,' they wrote.

'Now what on earth do they mean by that?' I asked Beryl suspiciously.

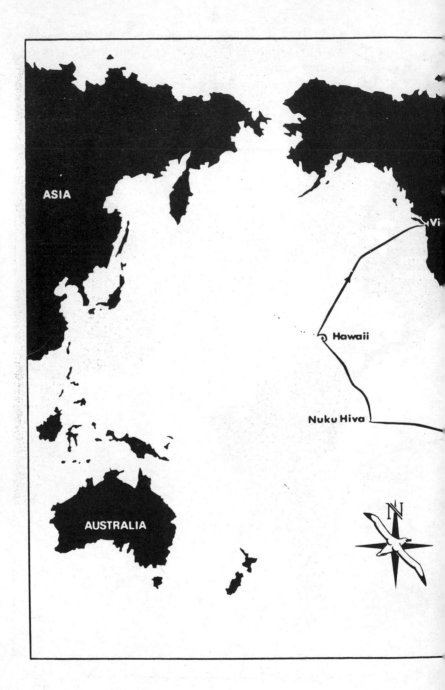

From Yarmouth in England to Victoria, British Columbia.

CHAPTER TWO

To Spain

Not even the ferry was stirring when we left Lymington—nor was the sun up—but a new day had come with a light wind from the west. We had our papers and had paid our bills, and were free to go. As a boy in the early morning may tiptoe down the stairs, shoes in hand, to smell the hawthorn and the may and feel the dew on his feet, so now *Tzu Hang* turned her head for the sea.

The yachts on either side of the river stood tall and silent, gravely watching her go and making no comment, the tide ripples began to show on the seaward side of the buoys, and small black crabs edged along the weed and rust at their sides. Gulls and terns flew singly overhead, silent and preoccupied, as if only half awake and still undecided about their destination. The murmur of *Tzu Hang*'s engine, the ripple of water, and the chatter of slides as we hoisted the sails, were the only sounds.

The yachts that we were passing grew larger and their spacing wider as we moved down river. The wind freshened and our sails filled. I could see the Jack in the Basket that marked the river mouth and stopped the motor. It looked as if we would have to beat down the Solent to clear the Needles, but as the tide strengthened *Tzu Hang* pointed up well on the starboard tack, and with everything taut and still, made off for the open sea.

It was the third time that we had sailed from England for Canada, each time not knowing whether *Tzu Hang* would come back again, so that each departure had had in it something of farewell. The first time we had sailed the regular trade-wind route, the second time east about, and now we were sailing for Cape Horn.

Although I had been a soldier and the son of a doctor, and Beryl's father and her brothers had been soldiers, we both had the sea in our pedigrees. Beryl was more liberally endowed with admirals than I, and sometimes seems almost too much aware of it, but I had an admiral on my mother's side. Beryl's grandfather was drowned in the tragic capsizing of H.M.S. *Captain*, but then I had an uncle, John Kendall, who was washed overboard and lost off Cape Horn. His painting used to hang in the study of my mother's home, a young man wearing a small gold-braided cap. He was second mate on a square-rigger and was caught by a wave when struggling into his oilskins, as he came too quickly on deck, answering a call for all hands. My grandfather also was master of a square-rigger before retiring to be a farmer. In my mother's family there was also a John Kendall who sailed with Lord Byron round the world in 1765 and was promoted from mate of the *Tamar* to second lieutenant of the *Dolphin* during the voyage. My brother inherited two small wall vases from his cabin. A Lieutenant Kendall of H.M.S. *Chanticleer* made the survey of Staten Island, I expect he was of the same family. We both had sailors in our ancestry, but in spite of Beryl's admirals, I thought that I had the edge on her in regard to Cape Horn. Perhaps something in our blood was sending us south.

By the evening we were approaching the traffic lane off the Casquets and tacked to avoid it, and by ten o'clock, with the radio treating us to Madame Melba's singing and then Toscanini conducting Verdi's *Requiem*, we saw the four flashes of the light on Portland Bill. At the same time next evening the Lizard light fell below the horizon. We were sailing with working jib and reefed main close-hauled for Ushant. Next morning the wind fell light and we continued on the same tack through fog and rain. The weather cleared in the evening and we went about to give Ushant a wider berth, but about midnight the wind had dropped and we rolled unhappily in the traffic lanes in dripping and impenetrable fog.

17

Far and near, desolate and threatening, came the moan of fog-horns, approaching, passing, and drawing away. It was my watch and I sat in the lonely cockpit, thinking of some benighted trapper in far northern woods, tending the last embers of his fire, listening to the call of distant wolves, and wondering whether they were following his trail. I do not know whether wolves will attack men, but I am sure no trapper ever listened to them more anxiously than we listened to the fog-horns that night.

We had our radar reflector rigged and angled so that it presented as many and varied surfaces to a beam as possible, but, although all ships would be using radar, I wondered whether they might not be watching bigger and better blips than ours. I tried the fog-horn but it had rusted and the pin stuck down. It screamed into the night, bringing Bob and Beryl rushing on to the deck, with various suggestions as to how to stop it, while I scrabbled at it and shook it with the same horrified embarrassment that a motorist feels when his horn has jammed. Presently the noise died to a whimper and, like a genie from a bottle, it was gone for ever. In the sudden silence that followed all the world seemed shocked and listening, then from far away came the distant moans of the hunting pack again.

We had taken down the jib and mizzen and hauled the mainsheet in taut, leaving the sail up, partly to steady our rolling and partly in the hopes that we might be better visible should a ship come upon us. It would have been a wise precaution to inflate the rubber dinghy and leave it loose on deck, but it was stowed away in the stern and I let Bob and Beryl turn in again without suggesting it. I sat there listening, listening beyond the immediate sounds, the rustle of water, the 'whup' of the sail as *Tzu Hang* rolled, the rattle of slides in the tracks, the patter of mist drops as they fell to the deck from rigging and booms, and the soft chink of a cup from down below. In the galley the light was turned down, so that it might not bother the eyes of the helmsman, but a helmsman might just as well have been blind on a night like this, for we were not moving and the best of eyes could see nothing. I could hear five separate fog-horns and now, just as the trapper might have shifted restlessly and stirred his fire, I sat up and took a rough bearing over the compass at the direction of a fog-horn that seemed nearer than before.

A few minutes later it sounded again, still on the same bearing but this time it seemed to be fainter. I adjusted the compass face and four minutes later heard it again, still on the same bearing and definitely more distinct and closer than before.

There is really little that one can do about this kind of situation except sit and sweat it out. To start the engine in order to be ready to move only drowns the noise of the approaching ship. To move is almost the worst thing to do for the ship may already have you in its radar and may be aiming to pass within half a cable or less. I tested the big flash-light. Its beams only lit the grey shroud about us, but the glow might show for a hundred yards. I went below and switched on the mast light. Perhaps the mist was thinner up there and the light could be seen from a ship's bridge but it looked a dim little glimmer from the cockpit. As I came back on deck I brought my hunting horn from its pocket inside the doghouse. John Peel's horn might bring folks from their bed, and mine was all right for calling the yacht club boat or persuading a bridge to open, but I had little faith that it would be heard far at sea.

The fog-horn sounded again. This time it had an eager panting sound behind the threat and again appeared to be on exactly the same bearing. I went below again and woke Deryl and Bob. 'I think you'd better be on deck,' I said. 'A ship seems to be heading our way.' They came up and we all sat listening. The horn sounded again. 'That's quite close,' said Bob. 'Let's light all the lights we've got,' said Beryl going below for another flash-light. By the time she was back we could hear the noise of a ship's engine and once again the shuddering roar of its horn.

'That's horribly close,' said Beryl, as we all stood up peering into the gloom shining two flash-lights up into the air. 'Hadn't you better blow your horn. I'm going to get Pwe and her life-belt.'

I licked my lips and blew. The thin note which sounds so far in woodland or across winter fields vanished feebly into the night. I blew again and again until my unpractised lips were numb. Then listened. We stood breathless, hearts beating, ready to jump if necessary. There was a rushing and a rumbling and clanking which seemed to stretch out ahead of the bow and past our stern. Then all at once there was the heavy beat of a ship's screw and the suck of her wash as the stern slid past us, yet we saw no glimmer of light nor sign of her at all.

'That was a close one,' said Bob, 'I don't want any more like that.'

'That was closer than the one off the Berlengas Islands,' said Beryl, referring to a previous experience.

'That's the closest we've ever had,' said I. 'I swear I heard an engineer put his coffee cup down.'

It was Bob's watch, and although the fog-horns continued to sound round us no other ship came close. Beryl, when she came up for her turn, found Bob sitting on the doghouse roof, clutching the hunting horn in his hand. As he went below he handed it to her. 'I don't want it,' she said. 'It's no good to me. I can't blow it.'

'You're kidding,' he said, looking at her in surprise.

'Why. Can you?' she asked.

'Of course,' he said, putting the horn to his lips and blowing mightily, but only achieving a gush of silent air. 'Well,' he said, 'I thought that all you had to do was to blow,' and disappeared below. Anyway, thought Beryl, it kept him happy just sitting there holding it.

By 0400 we were sailing again, still in fog, but soon we were done with it. We sailed westward most of that day, in order to get well clear of Ushant, and then turned southwards across the Bay of Biscay, never having seen Ushant nor any part of the French coast. We made a good crossing in warm weather so that Bob soon had his shirt off in an attempt to recoup his Florida tan. He has excellent eyes and is always alert on watch, so that he was continually calling our attention to shipping that Beryl and I had not seen. It was my first intimation that my long-distance sight was no longer as good as it had been. One day he called to us:

'Come and look at this. I can't make out what's going on. It looks as if there's a ship in trouble over there and another one is going to help it. You see the ship over there,' we screwed up our eyes and looked in the direction that he was pointing, 'well right in front there's another one which looks as if it's sinking. A yacht perhaps.' I got the glasses and had a look through them. What Bob had seen was a tanker going to the rescue of its own bow.

During the next few days we settled down into an easy routine of shipboard life, a routine that we would keep up when not in port for many months to come and which became the regular pattern of our life at sea. I do not think that our method of the division of watches is necessarily suitable for other crews of three, but it suited us, particularly during long nights or cold nights. The 24 hours were divided so that we had only two hours at night at a stretch, and three hours by day. Daylight watches are nothing. People are up and about, food is probably on the way, and they pass quickly. It is at night when they drag. Bob and I used to swap our watches round every week but Beryl liked to have hers at the same time throughout the voyage.

Most important, however, since we had such a long journey ahead of us, was that Beryl and I were getting accustomed to Bob, and he to us, for at sea there is no slipping away to the pub at the corner, or a neighbouring yacht, to relieve pent-up feelings. The crew is there for keeps or until port is made, but as far as Bob and ourselves were concerned there was no sign of pending friction. Perhaps he is a very tolerant person. The cat also had settled down and she and Bob were firm friends.

On August 25th at 0400, having sailed 660 miles in six days, we raised the light of Finisterre, after passing through numerous fishing boats and coastal shipping during the night. Presently we altered course down the coast for Arosa

Bay 30 miles to the southward. By the time *Tzu Hang* had sailed this distance, we were once more buried in fog. Although I knew that this sea fog was lying just across the entrance to the bay and that if I could find my way in we would soon be out of it, the coast here is so beset with rocks and variable currents that it is better to stay put, rather than grope one's way for the entrance. *Costa del Morte*, the Spaniards call it.

I could pick up the beacon on Finisterre 30 miles behind us and on Cabo Silliero 30 miles ahead, but neither of these showed me the entrance. From ashore there came a series of explosions of rockets, but in August any village in Spain is liable to be celebrating a fiesta, so that these were no guide. If I had known that Clio and Alex had driven down from the mountains to meet us and were then in Villa Garcia in sunlight looking towards the mouth of Rio Arosa, where they could see the fog lying, I might have attempted it. Instead we motored out westwards until we were between the hidden shore and the fog-horns on the shipping lane, and there we waited for the fog to lift. A big open fishing boat with a powerful motor came swirling past us and its crew looked at us in surprise before they vanished into the fog. They seemed to know exactly where they were, which was more than I did. The fog didn't lift and we settled down for another anxious night.

Early in the morning Beryl told me that she had heard the sound of breakers. They sounded some way off and I could still hear the fog-horns on the shipping lane and felt assured that we were better off where we were. Both Beryl and Bob are allergic to the sound of breakers—Bob particularly so since he has been wrecked on a coral reef—and soon I could hear them muttering together on the deck, but there was no wind and to them I remained annoyingly undisturbed.

Daylight came and presently Bob announced, with the air of one who had long been foretelling the worst and had now been proved correct, that there were rocks showing astern. The fog was beginning to lift and some jagged black rocks had appeared, the swell lipping and talking gently against them. They were not yet close enough to justify our getting under way and motoring seawards, where the fog was still thick, and this was just as well for as the fog lifted more rocks were disclosed to the westward. Presently the fog lifted completely and we were able to discover where we were. The tide during the night had carried us not into the Rio Arosa, as it might have done if we had been another mile farther down the coast, but into the rock-bound Corrubedo Bay, just north of the Isla Salvora, our turning point. We started the engine and, skirting these dark dangers that had been so close to us during the night, motored into the Rio Arosa, and were soon beating up with a fresh wind for Puerto Caraminal, where we anchored off the pier.

The most notable feature of Puerto Caraminal was the beach below the town which Beryl selected for me to meet her and Bob with the dinghy, in order to embark water, wine and stores. I rowed across to it while they set off to walk the length of the pier to the town. When I arrived at the beach I found that all the town drains emptied on to it, making a smell unique in horror, unique even in Spain. It was impossible to land on the slimy shore, so I stayed in the dinghy off the end of a long stone boat ramp. Down this came a frieze of bare-legged and black-dressed fisherwomen, balancing empty fish boxes on their heads with rough red hands. They waded into the water at the end of the ramp and washed the boxes in the sea as had been their custom perhaps for hundreds of years. They called to me as they did so, laughing loudly at some jest, but I could only guess at its savour. Presently Bob and Beryl arrived with their purchases and we made our way back to *Tzu Hang* and cleaner water as fast as the over-loaded dinghy would permit.

In the afternoon we sailed farther up the Rio Arosa and anchored off Punta Capitan after finding our way through a maze of mussel rigs, where there had only been one eight years before. There we had friends, the Borras family, who lived above the point, who never seemed to change, and whose hospitality never dimmed and had provided the highlight of each of our previous trips to Spain. Here Clio and Alex met us and drove Beryl and me to Piedrafita del Cebrero, where Alex was in charge of a new mining operation that was being started

23

by a Canadian company. Bob and Pwe remained in *Tzu Hang*.

Piedrafita del Cebrero is deep in the country and high in the hills above Lugo on the main road from Corunna to Madrid. Little has changed there in the past 200 years. In the morning the hills echoed with the shouts of men calling to their oxen as they ploughed the little fields on the steep hillsides, with wooden ploughs. Along the brows of the old bare hills kestrels wheel and hover. Dusty narrow roads cling to their edge, or dip to villages rich with the smell of dung and straw. Through this country Sir John Moore's army retreated before the French, to their evacuation by sea at Corunna.

I pictured it in the winter, snow on the hills and long files of mud-stained, footsore soldiers, the drunken and the dying stragglers, the exhausted women and children who followed an army if they could, the bullocks unable to pull the wagons of treasure which were pitched over the road near Piedrafita and down the hillside. An army defeated by retreat, whose troops still repulsed the enemy whenever they stood against him, an army whose morale had reached the lowest depths but which recovered immediately it was asked to fight.

Clio and Alex were staying in a *refugio* attached to an old church, which a dynamo of a priest, Don Elias, had restored. While we were there he had organized the village and help from neighbouring villages in a threshing. Everyone was busy. An old threshing machine hummed and shook, men forked straw on to a stack which children dragged to its foot, or carried sacks of new grain to the granary. Don Elias, in a beret, was everywhere. Did we want 20 dozen eggs, a side of bacon, two smoked hams? It could be arranged. Orders were issued on the spot, so much from one village, so much from another and two days later, when we left, we had them all. The newest of new-laid but unwashed eggs, for they keep best, and smoky bacon and hams that kept forever, or at least until they were eaten, and tasted better at sea than any hams or bacon had ever tasted ashore.

A week later we were ready to sail again. We had a final party on *Tzu Hang* at Punta Capitan. The cabin was full of

Borras men and women and their friends; of wine, cigarette smoke, a guitar and song, until they rowed away in darkness singing the haunting song of farewell:

> '*Adios con el corazon, que con el alma no puedo*
> *Al despedirme de ti*
> *Al despedirme ne muero.*
> *Tu seras el bien de mi vida,*
> *Tu seras el bien de mi alma,*
> *Tu seras el pajaro pinto que*
> *Alegre canta por las mananas.*

That is how Christina Borras wrote it in the log book.
How is this for a translation:

> Goodbye with my heart—but
>   not with my spirit
> At our parting
> Do not let memory die.
> You will be the good in my life,
> You will be the good in my spirit,
> You will be the blue bird
> That sings gay songs of the morrow.

CHAPTER THREE

To the Cape Verde Islands

The crew of a yacht making or contemplating ocean passages, finds itself willy-nilly involved in history. Sailing ships themselves are an anachronism and their once well populated ways are deserted now, so that the skipper or navigator of a small yacht when planning his route finds himself delving into the past and, in my case, too well aware that he doesn't know much about it.

What waste it is to sail into Quiberon Bay and not know about Hawke; to sail into Cadiz and not know how Drake singed the King of Spain's beard; or to sail between St Lucia and St Vincent and not be able to imagine Rodney cutting through the French line of battle, the thunder of the guns, the billowing smoke, and the bantam cock from a smashed chicken coop perched on the bulwark and crowing at every broadside.

It is to the sailing ship routes, the winds and currents, that a yachtsman's interest is first directed, and from these to the early navigators whose keels first ploughed them, and then to the events in history that marked them.

It is one of the rewards of sailing a yacht along the ocean passages of the world that it will make its landfalls not necessarily on the lighthouses, the buildings, and radio towers of modern development, but on some blue distant headland, a fringe of coconut trees, or a dark hill in the moonlight, just as they appeared to the old adventurers two or three hundred years ago. There is no longer the satisfaction of new discovery, but there is the satisfaction of knowing that so small a ship had made such a journey with so few to man it.

It was the 200th anniversary of the start of Captain James Cook's first voyage from England, through the Straits of Le Maire and round Cape Horn, and the day that we were waiting in fog off the Rio Arosa, the *Endeavour* in 1768, finding a fair wind, had sailed from Plymouth Sound. She was more than twice the length of *Tzu Hang*, nearly three times the beam, and she carried nearly 40 times as many in her complement. Cook sailed at the time of a sudden explosion of exploration in the Pacific that developed after the Seven Years' War, and a few years before him had gone Captain Byron, and Wallis and Carteret. We had the stories of their voyages on board. All took the same route, but only Cook went round the Horn, for after Lord Anson's voyage in 1741 the Horn was regarded as the ultimate in awfulness of the known ocean passages, particularly by Byron, who had made it in the *Wager*, one of Anson's squadron, later wrecked on the Patagonian shore. Cook appreciated the advantages of the weather shore provided by the islands terminating in Cape Horn itself, whereas the others feared this inhospitable coast almost as much as the westerly winds and preferred to go through the Straits of Magellan. As far as we were concerned, looking at a drawing of *Endeavour's* great bluff bows and square rig, if she could make the windward passage surely we could. *Endeavour* might have been able to stand up to heavier seas than we and to hold her position in the face of severe gales longer, but if the winds were not too strong to allow us to make to windward, surely we could do so better and faster than she.

Ships going south for the Straits of Magellan, or even bound for the Cape of Good Hope if the voyage had been long, had been accustomed to putting in to Rio de Janeiro for water and supplies, since the Spanish ports of South America at this time were closed to them. Whether bound for the Cape of Good Hope or the Straits of Magellan the first part of their route was the same. Owing to the west-setting South Equatorial Current and the south-east Trades, it was necessary to get as far south as possible before meeting them, in order to avoid being carried north of the north-east shoulder of South America. If this happened, rather than attempting to beat down the South American coast against wind and current, it was better to make a northerly circle back to where they had started from and to try again.

The route therefore lay from Madeira, where ships often re-victualled, south with the north-east Trades to the Cape Verde Islands to re-victual and water again at Porto Praia on Santiago, and then still south to about latitude 4°N, tacking if necessary towards the African coast rather than being persuaded to sail westward too soon, which would inevitably involve them in a harder battle with the south-east Trades. Nothing had changed in 200 years with regard to the courses, but as sailing ships had become larger and their crews smaller it had been no longer necessary to make the stops for provisioning and, if necessary, the ports of the River Plate were now open to them.

This then was our route. Like Byron, Wallis, Carteret, and Cook, we were bound for Porto Praia, and some of their experiences we would savour also. I wished that I had one of the vases from John Kendall's cabin to make the voyage a second time.

We sailed from the Isla Salvora, with its sheltered little anchorage watched over by a stone mermaid, on September 5th. The Portuguese Trades were on the whole light and variable, but there was plenty of sunshine and plenty of traffic to keep us interested, while Bob spent most of each day busily recovering his Florida tan, but this only when he was not trying to persuade *Tzu Hang* to sail faster. It was already obvious that he could not bear to have the twins set unless it was blowing what Lord Byron refers to even in these waters as a 'nice gale' for he always wanted her to carry as much sail as possible. Beryl and I soon realized that those easy days of slopping along while *Tzu Hang* sailed herself were gone. It wasn't that Bob said anything, but he just looked unhappy if we were not doing our best.

On September 11th we were becalmed about 30 miles from Puerto Santo and went overboard for a swim. The water was perfect and, when we looked down, had the colour and refraction of a star sapphire, so that shades of blue seemed to radiate from far below, and we, a little detached from *Tzu Hang*, floated over a blue immensity, like a glider along a cliff face. Back on board for lunch, we saw a ship approaching. She was the S.S. *Funchal* on her way to Madeira, loaded with tourists, and she altered course in order to pass close to us. I hoisted the signal 'WAY' (wish you a pleasant voyage), to which, to my great delight, she replied. The tourists crowded the rail, waving and whistling, and someone called to us, 'What are you waiting for?'

'The wind,' we shouted back.

In the night we could see Puerto Santo light but the wind was so faint that we could not lose it, and in the morning the 'Disneyland' outline of the island was visible. On this day we sailed close to the long jagged ridges of the Islas Desertas on the other side of which, sheltered from the Trade Winds, we had anchored on our first Atlantic crossing. Here Bob saw a small bird, also on a passage, fall into the water when he had only a few miles to go to safety. Even if you swim for them, as Beryl has done, it is impossible to save them. They have exhausted all their power and their will to live and will be dead and still within an hour or two. The only bird that we have been able to succour was a carrier-pigeon, which, being used to men, came on board while he was still strong enough to take water and food, and a pelican that had become entangled in a double fish-hook, which was caught in his bill and his wing, so that he could not fly. We have tried again and again with other exhausted birds of passage but, having saved them from the sea and the cat, they have died of exhaustion.

On September 13th Madeira was behind us. It was the day that 200 years ago *Endeavour* had anchored in Funchal roads, and Mr Wier, the master's mate, had been carried over by the anchor, with his foot caught in the buoy rope. The men at the capstan broke their backs to get him up again but he was drowned before they got him to the surface. It was also on this day in 1766 and in just about the exact position that we were sailing that the *Dolphin*, on her second circumnavigation, and the *Swallow* backed their topsails and Captain Wallis handed Captain Carteret his orders, telling him that he was to accompany him in a subordinate position on a voyage of discovery to the South Seas. Captain Carteret was enormously upset at this for not only was his ship unfit for such a task, but the *Dolphin* had all the trade goods on board, all the bosun's stores and was much the faster ship.

On September 14th we were approaching Palma, but the islands were buried in great banks of cloud and we saw none of them. During the night we saw lights ashore and although we passed through the Islands, that is all we saw of the Canaries. The following day we celebrated 1,000 miles on the log by a second drink before dinner, as is our custom for every 1,000 miles. Bob mixed the drinks so he should know why Beryl went below saying that it was time to 'sy the frausages'. We were ten days out but were satisfied with our progress since we had had little but light and variable winds. Next day we were into the north-east Trades and from then on made better time.

On September 18th a ship appeared on the horizon which looked as if it would pass about two miles away. There was a fresh Trade blowing and we had the main set and jib boomed out so that we were running fast. The ship altered course, passed close astern, and then made a 180° turn and steamed up alongside. She was called the *Cyril* and had a 'B' on her funnel. Beryl and I had a friend whom we had last heard of as mate of the *Basil*, of the Brocklebank line, which trades to Brazil. His name was Bill Crawley and he had helped us to paint *Tzu Hang* in Durban while waiting for his ship there. Now we wondered if he had been on board *Cyril*, for she had turned away again and left us.

'But we'd have recognized him,' said Beryl, 'they were close enough.'

'He could have used the loud-hailer—but then we were painted white when he knew us,' I said.

'He said he'd know us whatever colour we were painted,' said Beryl.

Eventually we had to give up the idea of such a coincidence. Bill Crawley had had many good tales to tell while he helped us in Durban. During the war he once shipped from Hull, where his home was and was bombed and sunk in the estuary of the Humber within an hour of leaving. He was home again for lunch.

'Well, whatever are you doing, lad?' asked his mother. 'There's nothing to eat. I thought you'd gone to work.'

'Gone to work!' said Bill, as he told us, indignant like, 'Gone to work! I'm a ruddy survivor.'

From the age of 14, when he left school, he had been a sailor. First in trawlers, then in the Navy, then in the Merchant Service, and now he had his Master's ticket. He knew what he was talking about with small boats too, for he had been sunk on the Murmansk convoy and sailed a lifeboat down to the north coast of Ireland, where he had been run down in the dark and subsequently picked up by a frigate.

On September 19th we were able to pick up the air beacon on Sal, the most northerly of the Cape Verde Islands, at about 100 miles on our small DF radio. Sights were difficult on account of the haze of African dust that filled the upper air and dimmed the horizon but gave us wonderful sunsets in compensation. While sitting comfortably and rather sleepily in the cockpit during my night watch I thought of the D'Oliviera controversy and the resulting cancellation of the cricket test matches with South Africa, which was in the news then. It made me think of cricket, of the smell of grass and the noise of a well-hit ball, when suddenly I was caught dreaming at first slip. A flying fish had hit me square in the stomach and almost knocked the breath out of my body.

There was still no sign of daylight, and the stars, if they showed at all through the haze of African dust, showed only directly overhead. As I looked up trying to distinguish those that I could see, two bright lights appeared close together moving swiftly across the sky immediately above me, but I could hear no sound. They threw an arc of golden light ahead of them, like a drawn bow, and this golden bow, moving so swiftly and silently across the sky had something so mysterious and miraculous about it, that I felt a great sense of uplift, as if it had vouchsafed for me to see this vision, not seen by other men. As I puzzled over it I remembered the air strip at Sal, 100 miles to the north, and decided, alas, that this was an aircraft already on its descent for Sal, testing its landing lights, and it was the dust in the air that they illuminated, which made this beautiful golden bow, moving so swiftly across the sky. For every unidentified flying object, there seems to be almost always a rational answer.

Next morning was spent in a navigational flurry as we could see no sign of the Islands although we were close to them, and from an early fix with the moon and Sirius, found that we had a strong north-westerly set. We saw nothing of Sal although the beacon told us that it was there, hidden in the deceptive haze. We set a course south along the east-coast of Buono Vista Island, and about 12 miles off shore by calculation, although there was no sign of the Island. A fresh Trade Wind blew all night and all three of us on our separate watches distinctly saw breakers to starboard, but fortunately not so distinctly as to justify waking the others, for they were only breaking crests after all. At about 0400, when I felt that we were well clear of the southern end of the island, we altered course westward for Maio.

Daylight came on September 21st, a golden hazy dawn and Beryl's birthday, but there was still no sign of the islands amongst which we were sailing. Just before lunch Maio materialized ahead, coming out of the haze as a shadowy outline and standing high, for we were only ten miles away. Soon it began to take on colour, a desert stony landscape, with only a few houses and a fort on the west side at Puerto Ingles. For the time being we could only see stony, arid hills, two lonely palm trees standing lost and hand in hand, a stone wall enclosing nothing but stones and jagged black rocks close in that guarded the shore. Perhaps there was some vegetation higher up and towards the north but we saw none of it, neither man, nor beast.

Once round the southern point the Trade Wind blew freshly

down the channel between the Islands and *Tzu Hang* went off with the bit in her teeth for Santiago and Porto Praia. For some time we could see nothing of Santiago only 20-odd miles away, but as Maio faded Santiago appeared. Soon we could see the south-western point which hides the entrance to Porto Praia and towards this we set our course. In 1764 Lord Byron wrote in his journal: 'July 27. Little wind and hazy. This morning made the Island of Sal. Saw several turtles upon the water and lowered the jolly boat to attempt to strike them, but they all went down before the boat could get near them. Saturday July 28. Little wind and sometimes calm. This morning very near the island of Buono Vista. A great swell from the South. Sunday July 29. Off the Island of Mai in the morning. Steered close in for the Island of St Jago, but were for some time at a loss for Porto Praia Bay, which after some hours search we found lay close round the south west point.'

As we rounded the south-west point we took down the mizzen, soon followed by the jib and sailed up the harbour under our main. A steamer was anchored in the roads and we continued past it towards a dilapidated schooner which we later discovered carried passengers to Dakar, a short trip of only 400 miles for £75 a ticket, and anchored there. We had sailed 1,860 miles in 16 days. Closer in still there was another small motor-ship apparently sinking, but to our surprise, after discharging a cargo of salt it got up its anchor, and, although still to our eyes in a sinking condition, puffed happily away. We had not been anchored long before the Port Captain and the International Police came on board, and, after each had had a glass of whisky, disappeared with our passports, a practice which never fails to annoy, especially here, where a southerly wind might cause us to leave in a hurry. 'The anchorage is safe in the dry season, from December until June inclusive, for ships of any size,' says *The Africa Pilot*, 'but during the rainy season the wind occasionally sets in strongly with a heavy swell and short sea, which render it unsafe for sailing vessels. Sailing vessels from July to September should anchor well outside in 17 fathoms.' Both the *Dolphin* in 1764 and *Tzu Hang* in 1968 anchored in eight fathoms, about a quarter of a mile from the shore, but we were both equally anxious to get on our stores and to get away.

We saw the International Police and our passports off with mixed feelings and settled down to celebrate Beryl's birthday with a bottle of champagne. The cork hit the deck-head with such a flurry of foam that the cat thought another flying fish had arrived on board and hurried off to retrieve it.

Next day we all went ashore in the dinghy. It was impossible to leave it in the water because of the swell, but there were at least 50 naked little black boys waiting to welcome us, who carried the dinghy above their heads to the foot of the pier, and who crowded round us, plucking at our sleeves and trousers, demanding not money but attention. In order to get away from such a crowd, and Beryl having discovered a well-dressed young man called Carlos who was eager to be her guide, we got a taxi and drove up the hill to the market.

Beryl soon had her marketing face on, when she hunts and pries and fingers and nothing will distract her. She is unaware of heat and smells or the curiosity of the natives who crowd around her, only determined to complete her list at the best prices. She does not enjoy shopping but she tackles it in the same way that she tackles any other job, with energy and application. Soon she was in a dark little shop tasting the local imported Portuguese wine, unable to bring herself to buy— with good reason since it was outrageously expensive. 'It's really quite good,' she said, as she handed a glass for Bob and me to try. We knew that we would have to have it and called it 'nigger wine', but down south, when it was heated with nutmeg and cinnamon it was really excellent. Meanwhile, the black storekeeper was laboriously pouring rice for her into empty wine bottles from a brown paper funnel.

I do not like crowds and I am unhappy with flies and with squalor. Porto Praia had them all and was unbearably hot into the bargain. I agreed with an earlier visitor in 1806 who wrote, 'Lovely and tempting as the land appeared, nothing can be more fallacious than the idea that going ashore tends to invigorate a white man.' Beryl was as energetic as ever but for me the journey reached its nadir in the meat market where the remaining scraps were already on their way to decomposition, and its apogee as we went down the hill to the goal of *Tzu Hang*, rest, coolness and cleanliness. On the way we met a black girl carrying crayfish, two of which we bought. They were still alive, but feeble. At the bottom of the hill we found a lorry outside the Harbourmaster's office loaded with 40-gallon drums which were being filled with water.

'For you,' they said.

'But how much are you giving us?'

'Two tons.'

'But we can only take 40 gallons.'

Eventually we settled for two drums, since these were already filled. They drove them to the pier head and lowered them by a hand-operated crane to a heavy rowing boat. A big surf was running, and Bob, already beginning to look after us ashore with a filial regard as if we were sporting, but not altogether competent, parents, said, 'You two go with the water and I'll take the dinghy.'

I knew that he was thinking of the surf, so immediately said that I would take the dinghy. It was already launched by the time we had got down the steps and I got in successfully as it rose on the swell.

'Chuck me the crayfish,' I called and no sooner were they on board than a swell broke and plucked me away from the man who was holding the painter. The next moment I was riding the crest of the wave, foaming towards the shore, conscious of Bob's horrified look as I left him at a speed that seemed to be well over 30 miles an hour.

The concrete supports of the pier flashed past me so that I felt I was on the race-track at Monza. I knew that I had to do something or else we were going to strike one and tried to heel the dinghy away. It seemed to have the opposite effect. We charged in and the next moment were rolling head over heels, dinghy, oars, and crayfish, all pursuing our own routes through the surf.

If I had tried to escape from black hands, there were now a hundred waiting to receive me and I was mobbed by shining black bodies, all as naked as needles, who recovered me, oars, dinghy, and crayfish and finally launched us again through the surf. Since they swam like fish I soon had them all clinging to the dinghy again, and had to prise them off ungratefully before I could row back to the boat.

Meanwhile, Bob, running up the steps, called to Beryl, 'He's gone in, a wave took him ashore.'

Beryl, seeing his worried face, called 'Don't worry. He's always doing things like that. He'll be perfectly all right.'

Bob ran down the pier, and then, seeing that I was indeed all right, walked back with his attendant swarm. During the passage to Porto Praia he had won back his tan. Now he heard them discussing us as they walked down the pier. Bob had picked up enough Portuguese in Rio to understand. 'The old ones,' they said, 'they are white. But the young one, he's half-coloured.'

Next day was spent in getting stores on board and swimming, for it was extremely hot. We got back our passports and entertained the Harbourmaster and his plump little daughter, Louisa. The swell rolled in and neither of them were seasick and in the Fort above the bugles sounded. The same writer who told of the fallacy of benefits gained by going ashore, described the arrival of a British fleet in Porto Praia in 1806, on its way to Capetown.

'Upon our arrival the garrison attempted to salute the British flag. With the exception of a monstrous three cocked sombrero, the soldiers were perfectly naked, and a long pole of hardwood with a bayonet upon it, formed the only weapon with which the major part were armed. About twenty old cannon ranged in line above us on the esplanade were fired by a match on the end of a long pole. The cannoneer ran away at each discharge and the carriage invariably upset, but being quite rotten became useless.'

Things have changed much, but in Porto Praia perhaps not so much after all in 200 years. Byron wrote: 'We found the watering very inconvenient from the great surf upon the shore, as well as being forced to roll our cask at some distance from the beach to a dirty muddy well. I procured three bullocks for the people, but they were little better than carrion, and the weather so excessively hot, that the meat stunk in a few hours after being killed.'

Above us there were still old cannons upon the esplanade, although the soldiers in the fort were rather better dressed than in 1806, our meat was stinking even before Beryl had time to cook it, and our water turned green before we arrived in Montevideo.

CHAPTER FOUR

Across the Atlantic to Montevideo

The sun rose above the fort on the morning of September
24th, as the bugles sounded a belated call for sleepy Portuguese
soldiers. It threw the shadow of the hill across the bay to the
Ilheu Santa Marcia, where lighters and fishing boats were
anchored. Its rays caught the top of *Tzu Hang*'s mast and, as
if this was a signal, several small fishing boats, each manned
by two men, were rowed out to her. The first tied to *Tzu
Hang*'s side, and several others to this one, lying in a row, side
by side. While we were at breakfast the soft rumble of the
men's voices came to us.

They were catching fish for bait from the shoal of small fry
that always lay in the shade of *Tzu Hang*'s side, flicking them
out of the water with twigs to which were attached a yard of
thin nylon line and a small hook. Their faces were as black and
furrowed with age and weather as the sides of a volcano. They
talked quietly as if all the world was at peace and they half
asleep. While they talked, they jerked out the little fish, un-
hooked them and dropped them in the bottom of the boat, with
a movement so automatic that they seemed to be unaware of
any physical action. They stayed there for half an hour and
then moved off seawards, hoisting patched sails to the last of
the land breeze.

By then the first horde of naked little boys had swum out to
the anchored lighters. Soon they were diving and splashing,
bubbling and laughing and there they would spend most of the
day, apparently without the need of food. Beryl's factotum, the
brown-skinned Carlos, who spoke French since he was born in

38

Dakar, rowed out to say good-bye. He brought some special sausages that had been prepared by a friend of his, a 'noir', and which reeked of garlic.

Meanwhile the small breeze had dropped and the sun drove us into the sea for a swim. The water was fresh and cool and *Tzu Hang* rolled placidly above us, ready to go, playing with her anchor chain. Back on board we brought up the anchor and hoisted the sails, but they hung empty with no breath of wind to move us. I started the motor and almost immediately the Trade Wind, blowing freshly round Punta das Bicudas, reached into the bay. *Tzu Hang* heeled and her pace quickened. As we sailed out I thought of Wallis' squadron lying there on that same day in 1766, sails stowed on the yards, their yellow and black paint still fresh from England, the *Dolphin*, the *Swallow*, and a supply ship, with their boats ashore bringing water from the same spring that had served us.

Tzu Hang's wake was soon creaming behind her as we ran, still in shallow water, past the tall and venerable lighthouse off Punta Temerosa, the southern point of the island, past some of the fishing boats at anchor, disappearing and appearing in the trough of the sea, lying to wind and tide on frail, knotted anchor ropes. We sailed through the scattered boats into dark blue water and soon boats, lighthouse, and the island itself had vanished into the haze.

Next day the wind was light and we were for ever changing sail, with the staysail boomed out first on one side and then on the other. For a long time we sailed through, or were accompanied by, a large shoal of tunny. They were breaking water near the boat, lazily showing the scimitar-shaped dorsal fin and the top of their tail, so that it looked as if they had two narrow dorsal fins.

Our object now was to reach a point at 5°N and 20°W, and from there to take the best course to the equator with the intention of crossing between Longitudes 24° and 29°W, but the farther east within these limits, the better. From there we intended to stand directly through the south-east Trades towards Montevideo. This is the recommended sailing-ship course for this time of the year. We expected to have the north-east Trades until we reached the inter-tropical convergence zone, in other words, the Doldrums, and south of this to meet the southerly or south-westerly winds of the African monsoon, until west of 20°W.

September 26th was another day of light winds, but as the sky was overcast it was not so hot as the day before. Pwe was off her food and had a badly swollen face which a joint consultation of all the veterinarians on board attributed to an infected sinus. She had a very discoloured eye-tooth which looked as if it should come out, but the swelling went down after dosing her with powdered sulphonamide tablets in milk. The day of extraction was eventually postponed until we arrived in port, but her tooth continued to bother her at intervals for the rest of this part of the voyage.

During the night the wind freshened and we made good time but in the morning we found that we were far short of our dead reckoning position, having run into a north-setting current. A school of grampuses joined us during the day, and sometimes one of them would stand upright on its tail, its head about four feet out of the water. During the night there was one still with us, breathing heavily.

> 'We are Grampus Griseus,' he lisped odorously,
> And nothing can dismay us
> But the plural of the generic noun "Grampus",
> Are we Grampi or Grampuses
> That is what confuses
> Intelligent, cetaceans
> Such as us.'

In night-watch madness I imagined him standing on his tail and singing this song.

We were passing through many tide-rips, showing that we were still on the edge of the north-setting current that had been holding us back, a branch of the counter-equatorial current that would soon be pushing us to the eastward. A big counter-current does not run in a solid stream but in branches like a

river estuary flowing between mud flats. A yacht is very suscept-
ible to currents since it moves so slowly, and the closer I have
been associated with them the more I have come to distrust
them. Even the most reliable can overrun themselves and flow
in the opposite direction, and wherever there is a strong current
there is usually a counter-current somewhere near.

These were hot windless days following one after the other
and we often made use of the motor but in compensation we
were able to go over the side for a swim. On the night of
September 27th there was lightning all across the southern sky.
All night it flickered and leapt, leaving no point free for long.
The morning brought real Doldrum weather, with an oily
grey sea and distant rain squalls dragging across the horizon.
Two swallows came on board; poor little people, so far from
land—400 miles—so hopelessly astray. A black night followed
and a black sea, slowly heaving. *Tzu Hang* was sailing herself,
quickening as the rain squalls drifted over her, but by four
o'clock in the morning there was no wind left and we had to
turn again to the motor. As daylight came Jupiter appeared for
the first time very low above the sun, the herald of a spectacular
daybreak.

All about us there was a glassy sea, rolling and writhing as if
in colic. Above us and around us there were Himalayas of
cloud, with one Everest that climbed to perhaps 12,000 feet,
from its black weeping base to the snow plume at its peak, just
now touched by the sun. I imagined myself ski-ing on its slopes
or flying an aircraft through great halls and passages of cloud.
Presently a wind blew the edges of the clouds upwards, an
up-current dragging them as if with a comb, so that the clouds
seemed to be brushing their hair. We were sailing again but
with only a light breeze and an occasional sprinkle of rain and
the dark cloud bases seemed to pick their way round us, emptying themselves in a continuous downpour which never seemed
to affect the density of the cloud above.

Our first two swallows had not stopped long but now we had
another on board. It settled on Bob's head, and when he
brushed it off in surprise, flew forward and down the forepeak

hatch. Beryl chased it away from there, for the cat was after it, but it fluttered in through the after-hatch and settled on my head. From there it flew to the top of the ship's clock, and having found an undisturbed perch, it started to twitter happily as if it was under the eaves of a house. The cat heard it and took up her watch below it on the chart table, so we took it on deck and put it under the dinghy, where it was at least safe from her. After a time it waddled out and attempted to fly away, but its wings must have stiffened after such a long flight, for it pitched into the sea. So much beauty and futility seemed concentrated in its little body, so much courage and despair.

On October 1st we ran into our first real rain squall when we flew along under all sail and a deluge of rain. The sea was quite flattened by it, wrinkled like an old whale's hide, and all pitted with drops. From each pit a new drop sprang and was momentarily suspended, so that the sea was covered with a myriad tiny fountains. The water cascaded from the booms like a stream over a weir and the deck was awash. The only suitable dress for the helmsman was bathing shorts, which we wore, anyway, all day, but the wind and the rain soon set him to shivering so that he called for his oilskin and dragged it on over his streaming skin. When at last we burst out of the rain, the wind left us wallowing in so erratic a sea that we took down all sail except the main and started the engine again.

We still had found no constant south wind. Squalls came rolling up from the south in long lines, but fizzled away into nothing, and the sky remained overcast with light rain and heavy showers. On October 3rd I wrote in the log, 'Almost the worst day I have ever had at sea. Big sea, no wind, continuous downpour, everything is soaking.' Even Bob began to show signs of gloom.

'I've got a leak in my bunk right over my head,' he said lugubriously.

'Can't you move down?' Beryl suggested.

'I've got one over my feet too,' he said. 'Can't fix anything until we get some dry weather. My brother took eighteen days to get through the Doldrums.'

He brightened up when he saw a large shark following us. It had a remora attached to it as well as being accompanied by a pilot fish and had an ugly wound near its tail. It looked no happier than we.

The bad times in *Tzu Hang* are usually when she is becalmed and the sea is rough, from some distant disturbance, when the skies are grey, and it looks as if there is no reason why the wind should ever blow again from a favourable direction. It is then that I begin to think of the amount of water that we have or the remaining gallons of fuel. As so often happens at sea, when everything is at its worst a change comes for the good; hope and enthusiasm prevail where a moment before there was black— but silent—despair. The change came now with a southerly wind. We went on the port tack and sailed into clearing skies, leaving Africa and the dreary monsoon behind us. Next day with the wind in the south-east we were on our way for the equator and south to Montevideo. The south-east Trade did not come all at once, but from now on it steadied and improved. For the first day or two we tacked to avoid squalls or tacked perforce because of the temporary change in the wind that accompanied them. Up to now we had averaged only 76 miles a day, in spite of making plenty of use of the motor to help us through the Doldrums, but now our mileage began to increase, although we were still meeting an east-going current.

On October 6th we were 2° 12′N at noon. I relieved Bob at midnight. He had a cup of cocoa ready for me, so that the watch started well. I sat in the cockpit drinking it, coming slowly fully awake. A full moon and high cloud with the wind in the south-east. The clouds covered the sky, a thin covering, shining white in the moonlight, with here and there a large crack showing like a crevasse on snow-fields, the sky blue-black behind. The mainsail we had had made in Japan, had developed a flutter in the leach, and now that we were close-hauled this insistent 'phut, phut, phut', had become one of our noises, like a clink from the galley, the tap of a jib block on the deck, or the cat's complaint as her bed companion of the moment turned over in the bunk. We were sailing quietly at about three and a half knots, the

43

night warm about us, so that a shirt and shorts were all the clothing necessary on watch. I could hear a steady 'shush, shush', from the bow, and the trickle of water, like a running tap along *Tzu Hang*'s side. A bird was flying round us and calling. I could see it at times, a fleeting shadow against the white cloud, and wondered if it was one of the white-tailed tropic birds that we had seen in the afternoon.

Pwe arrived on deck, materializing suddenly by my side. Presently she hopped over the cockpit combing and started her flying fish patrol up the starboard rail, leaning to the roll of the ship. Halfway up she stopped and called. Whether this is to give herself courage or to frighten flying fish on to the deck, only she can tell, but it is a noise that you would expect a leopard to make and not a small cat. 'Stop it,' I hissed at her, and eventually she stopped her yelling and tottered off on her inadequate legs, looking as if she might be swept overboard at any moment. Should she spot a flying fish on the deck she would move like a flash to catch it. She always makes two complete tours and then pauses at the hatch as if about to go below. She invariably reconsiders this decision as if she cannot believe that there is no fish there and makes a third tour. When she returns empty-handed for the third time she goes below and informs everyone of her disappointment. Should by any chance a sleeper not have awakened she will then join him in his bunk, tramping all over him to ensure he may appreciate the honour of her choice.

The following night, I thought, we should be across the equator. We had checked the journals of the old discoverers that we had on board. Wallis' time to the Line was not mentioned, but Cook was off Buono Vista in the Cape Verdes on September 29th and crossed the Line on October 25th. Byron left Porto Praia on August 2nd and crossed the Line on August 25th/26th. *Tzu Hang*, with the help of her motor, took 14 days. Presently our routes would diverge because they all called at Rio de Janeiro for supplies. Amongst our books we also had Captain Bestic's great story of the *Denbigh Castle*, a full-rigged ship on a voyage to Mollendo in Chile. Her mainmast was nearly four times as tall as *Tzu Hang*'s and she was six times as long. She was off Staten Island in December 1908 and three months later was still trying to round the Horn. She gave up the attempt and sailed to Chile by way of Australia instead. The author put down her failure to her Captain being over 60 and no longer having the nerve to carry sail when it was needed, to force a rapid doubling of the Cape when he had the chance. It was good reading for me, but perhaps not the best for Bob.

Next night the bird was round again and proved to be a noddy, a black tern with a white forehead. On several occasions these terns have tried to board *Tzu Hang* at night. On Beryl's watch they nearly drove the cat mad with excitement so that Beryl thought she might fall into the sea while trying to catch it. Eventually she hit it with the cat's brush and it fell into the sea, recovered itself and thereafter kept its distance. The following night a noddy was back again and settled on Bob's head. His hair seemed to attract birds, or perhaps his quiet manner.

On October 7th we were well into the South Equatorial Current which on this day and the following gave us 30 miles in the right direction. Bob began to speculate on his chances of winning the bets that we had made on the length of our passage, worst loser to pay for a dinner in Montevideo. His estimate was the most optimistic but his hopes received a set-back when the rigging screw securing the forestay carried away. It was a massive bronze affair from some other ship, but too long for the forestay, so that it was fastened directly to the bow fitting without a shackle. I thought that there was sufficient play in the fitting, but it had obviously been too constricted and the metal of the screw had fatigued. Forestay, genoa and rigging screw were all streaming in the wind, but although Bob and Beryl had the sail down in no time it was so badly torn that we decided to postpone its repair until we arrived in Montevideo. Almost everything is duplicated in *Tzu Hang*, and her jib stay was set up hard, so that there was no great strain on the mast when the rigging screw on the forestay let go.

On this day we saw our first ship since leaving Porto Praia when a big tanker hove up over the horizon and passed close ahead of us on a north-north-westerly course. She was named *British Destiny*, and she drove past us, symbolically powerful and assured, on a dead straight course, certain of her goal. On this day also we celebrated our 1,000 miles from Porto Praia, with a second drink before dinner.

Six o'clock in the evening, all three of us on deck and the sun just dipped below the horizon;

'Here's to *Tzu Hang*,' I said, lifting my stainless steel mug, 'may she make a good passage round the Horn.'

'She's all right, it's the people in her, as Bill Tilman says,' said Beryl, raising her mug.

'I can tell you,' said Bob, after drinking to *Tzu Hang*, 'If I had any doubts about her I wouldn't be on her. I wouldn't like to do it this way in a light displacement yacht, but she's got the weight and the strength you need for a passage to windward. She's still fast enough not to spend too long down there. I'm sure getting round quickly is half the battle.'

'I wonder if we'll meet any singlehanders?' I said.

'We might meet the one on the news last night who has just passed Melbourne.'

'I wonder if they'll have a press aircraft out looking for them like they did for Chichester. It would puzzle them if they spotted *Tzu Hang* going in the opposite direction,' said Beryl.

'We could black our faces and call ourselves *African Destiny*,' I said, thinking of the ship that we had seen in the morning. 'We could paint it on the canvas dodgers. If the press spotted that it would fairly put the cat amongst the pigeons.'

'We might hoist a signal,' suggested Bob, 'saying, "Is this the right way?"'

'It's a pity we aren't nearer to the Rocas Sao Paulo,' I said—these rocks lie in position 0° 56′N and 29°W—'we might find a singlehander just holed up there until it was time for him to start back to England. There's a safe cove 56 yards wide at the entrance and 100 yards long, with five to ten fathoms, completely sheltered.'

'We might find it full of them,' said Beryl.

The sea and clouds were darkening as we sat there in the cockpit, lazily enjoying the end of the day and our second drink, Beryl a rum sour, Bob a whisky sour, and I a gin sour to keep the scurvy at bay.

On October 11th a gannet appeared, the nearest land being the island of Fernando Noronha, 270 miles away, and we picked up Brazil on the broadcast band of the radio. *Tzu Hang* was making great strides now and the noon log for the past few days had read 1,188, 1,326, 1,451 and 1,584, but by observation we had made 450 miles, so that we had been helped by the current to the extent of 18 miles a day. On the whole the Trade Wind was light and day followed day, one much like the other, sunshine and cloud, blue skies and sparkling seas, and fleeting shadows. *Tzu Hang* rushed on eagerly and seemed to need no rest. Never was there a ship that had so evident a spirit of her own. We could feel that she was keen to get south. There is something about a wooden ship, fashioned from living wood by careful carpenters' hands, that no steel or plastic ship will ever wholly attain. The moon waxed and waned but we saw no other ship, only endless sea. Our mileage from October 12th by log was 1,706, 1,844, 1,980, and 2,108, but now we were no longer getting the same help from the current.

On the morning of October 18th we were down to 19° 30′S and 300 miles off shore. We could pick up the Victoria beacon, 200 miles north of Rio de Janeiro and due west of us. We kept outside Jaseur Bank, hoping for a better current which I thought might be deflected by the banks which run south from the Abrollos and out to Jaseur, but found no benefit. The wind fell very light in the morning and I suspected that we were running out of the Trades. Next day the wind was from the north-west, switching to south-west in the afternoon as a front passed over us and the Trades were gone. On the south-west wind, as if to mark their departure, there came a huge dark butterfly with long tails to his wings. I thought it was a large bat as it turned up astern of us and tried to come on board, but we were close-hauled, and although it got within a few feet of the stern it could not make it. Just as I realized that this was not a bat but the biggest butterfly that I had ever seen, and might have luffed up to let him on board, the wind from the sail caught it and it fell away to leeward and gave up the chase.

During the night I woke up and saw Beryl in her bunk beside me, curled up, the cat sitting on top of her, ears pricked, solemnly keeping her own hopeful watch for the sound of a fish on the deck. Bob's watch, I thought, and rolled out of my bunk to walk aft and have a word with him, and find out how we were doing. He was not in the cockpit. *Tzu Hang* was sailing by herself and the torch was rolling backwards and forwards across the deck inside the combing. It was the sight of this rolling torch—so unlike Bob to leave anything unattended—that caused me sudden anxiety. I caught it, switched it on, and searched forward along the deck. There was no sign of him. I hurried below feeling the fingers of fear clutch at me as I went, and shone the light into his bunk. He was sound asleep.

'Bob. Wake up, man. Bob.' What relief there was in my voice!

'Ugh,' said Bob, in his familiar bright way when roused.

'Your watch, Bob.'

He was already half out of his bunk. 'Didn't Beryl wake me?' he asked when he saw the time, 'I must have dropped off again.'

She had done so and heard him grunt, but since *Tzu Hang* was sailing herself, had not waited to see him out or made sure that he was properly awake. I was so relieved to see him there that I would have cheerfully finished the watch for him. The year before one of Bill Tilman's crew in *Mischief*, also on her way to Montevideo, had disappeared during his watch, unaccountably, in a Trade Wind sea, when everyone else was in his bunk below.

Next day we had a large swell from the south and a light wind. *Tzu Hang* climbed slowly up the slopes of the waves and then ducked quickly over their crest. Bob and Beryl saw a whale passing close to the ship on a northerly course. It broke water several times, although they did not see it blow. Then it sounded, so it had apparently recharged with sufficient oxygen before they saw it. We also had two land birds on board, a small green swallow and a grey bird about the size of a thrush with a forked tail and a black cap. Neither of them stayed long, but I doubt if they knew where they were going.

On October 22nd, our 28th day at sea, in latitude 24° 30'S, we saw our first albatross. A blood-red sunrise and a grey sea, a big swell and a light wind, and the great bird came swinging past us, aloof and haughty, not even deigning to stare. He gave me the same thrill that the aircraft lights, that golden bow, had done south of Buono Vista, and I felt uplifted by the sight of him, as if there was something of the miraculous in him. From now on we had all kinds of albatrosses, giant petrels, shear-waters and cape pigeons with us, but though they are always interesting to watch, there is nothing like the first wandering albatross, the biggest and the best of all albatrosses, particularly if you are in a small yacht and are heading deep into their domain.

Two days later we had a strong north-east wind. We handed the main for repairs and when we had it down found that there was a considerable amount of stitching to be renewed along the seams. While this was going on *Tzu Hang* continued under twins with a rising glass and the wind backing. Towards evening the shackle-pin on one of the clews let go and the boom fell into the water. The strain of its dragging against the shroud was too much for it and both the spar itself and the fitting at the mast cracked. This was not too bad a blow because this was almost the first time that we had had both twins up together, preferring always to use the main and one of the twins, since we had three watchkeepers. We set the main again, with one twin boomed out and continued like this all night.

Midnight found us sailing in a dank mist with a high glass, and this continued until noon next day with everything alow and aloft dripping. Then a front came through, bringing a fresh wind and clearing. skies. By 1400 we had reefed the main, followed by the mizzen, and by 2000 were sailing fast in a rough sea with a deep-reef rolled down in the main and the mizzen down. By midnight the wind had gone to the east and the glass was rising. Gone were the days of sunshine, steady wind, and steady glass. Now we were busy changing sail every few hours.

Out came jerseys and oilskins and we kept one eye open to weather and another on the glass.

On the morning of October 29th *Tzu Hang* was 120 miles off the entrance to the River Plate and we hoped to be in Montevideo by the following evening. Bob had brought a little wind man, a type of gremlin, with him from *Carronade*, known as 'Hughie', who sat on the upper crosstrees and kept a sharp ear cocked for any optimistic statement about the wind, without reference to him. To say 'If this wind holds, we'll be in Montevideo by tomorrow evening', was madness, unless we remembered to add, 'if Hughie agrees', or 'if Hughie is kind to us'. I was probably the culprit, as Beryl is usually pessimistic and Bob, from long association with Hughie, remembers either to propitiate him, or to keep his mouth shut.

At any rate Hughie was put out about something, and sent us a strong north-west wind. We managed to make 60 miles in the right direction, but this so infuriated him that he blew it up to gale force from the west and we were forced to heave to. He kept us there for most of the following day almost within spitting distance, it seemed to us after so long a passage, of our goal. In the evening a dove flew round the ship and although it carried no olive twig we decided that it was a signal to get going. We had been hove to under the main, and now it was in need of repair again. We had to make sail under the trysail, a very small sail, so that we could not take full advantage of the respite that Hughie had given us. He made a note of it.

Lord Byron also had his troubles on the same day and in the same place. He wrote in his journal: 'October 29. Wind shifted to the north west and blew a perfect storm with a most terrible sea. At eleven shifted to west south west still blowing as hard as ever. The ship laboured much, to ease her I ordered two fore and two aftermost guns to be thrown overboard. . . . Tues. Oct. 30, P.M. wind south west, blowing very hard until night and at 7 a.m. shifted to south by west. We had lain from the time the gale came on until 9 A.M. under a double reefed mainsail, then made sail and stood to the westward.' The gale seemed almost identical with ours, although perhaps a little stronger. 'Foul

50

weather Jack' never understated the weather conditions. Perhaps Hughie's ancestor was with him too.

October 31st came in with a fresh north-east breeze and glorious sailing. I felt confident that our trials were now over, but Bob had no faith in the River Plate. 'I've never moved in it without something awful blowing up,' he said. 'We came in in a gale in *Carronade*, and we came down from Buenos Aires in a gale. The channels are narrow and the buoys are not always where they are supposed to be. You'd better keep your fingers crossed until you are safe in harbour.' Bob had a great regard for the Argentinian and Uruguayan yachtsmen, not only for hospitality that *Carronade* had received, but for the sang-froid with which they sailed in these stormy waters.

Today, however, was perfect. The sun shone as the blue of the Atlantic turned to the green of the entrance and every sea-bird in creation seemed to be wheeling round us. Byron too remarked on them: 'For these past four days,' he wrote, 'abundance of birds about the ship. Some of immense size, brown and white, others as large and quite black, and a great many pentados, which are something larger than a pigeon, black and white spotted.' They were, I suppose, albatrosses, giant petrels, and cape pigeons.

Next morning a cluster of tall buildings appeared on the horizon, which Bob identified as Punta Del Este, and presently we discovered the lighthouse on the Isla de Lobos, with a couple of wrecks on the sand-banks near. We sailed through the channel between the Island and the mainland.

'Look at that sky,' Bob said. 'It looks wild.'

Above us white clouds were splashed here and there on a black background, as if an artist was painting on a huge canvas an abstract picture of strife and turmoil, sloshing it on but giving no indication as yet of how it might evolve. It looked as if there were two weather systems in conflict up there, and it certainly looked wild, but we were so near port that I could not feel worried.

'You've just got a thing about the Plate,' I said to Bob. 'We'll be in long before anything happens.'

'I've got a thing about it all right,' said Bob. 'I don't trust it.'

He was right. About four o'clock, sailing with the wind right aft and only the main set, a sudden gust of wind from the opposite direction set the sail shaking. We hauled it in and in a moment were hard-pressed in driving rain. There was no warning of this change, no sausage roll of cloud that heralds a *pampero*. It was just that the dark cloud ahead with rain below that had appeared to be moving with us, had reversed its direction. The thunder rolled above us as we reefed, the rain cascaded down, and the wind threatened to tear the jib and mizzen from their ties. We stuffed the jib down the fore hatch and doubly secured the mizzen. As gust after gust hit us I felt the huge estuary of the Plate shrinking to the size of a lake. Visibility was almost nil. We rolled another deep reef in the main.

The wind shifted to the south-east. If we chose to run now we would soon be up to English Bank and the constricted waters about Montevideo, but I preferred to wait for better weather. We were over 20 miles from English Bank, the wide stretch of shoals off the harbour, and I knew that if we took down all sail it would take us about 12 hours to drift there. We brought down the main and lashed it securely to the boom. Soon I began to wonder whether indeed we could carry any sail if we wanted to set it again. The helm was lashed down, with *Tzu Hang* on the port tack, so that she would then work her way to the north-west. I am absolutely against lying a-hull like this in heavy breaking seas, but this was an occasion when it could be done in safety. The wind was gusting to force 9 but the waves were not dangerous, running about ten feet high only. Our chief problem was where and how far we would drift.

All through the night *Tzu Hang* drifted roughly on her course on each side of the shipping lane. All through the night the thunder wrangled above us, the rain whipped our faces as we sat on watch, and the wind plucked at the furled sails. The seas came racing up, hissing at us, but the shallow water prevented them from building up dangerously. For the first time in our experience St Elmo's fire made a green glow at the mast head and at the ends of the cross-trees. From time to time we saw a haze of light through the driving rain, as some big ship trod her way cautiously in or out of the channel. Then we would wear ship to correct our position in relation to the shipping channel, and if it appeared that it might be necessary to take avoiding action, we turned *Tzu Hang*'s bow down wind so that she had enough speed to control her.

The thunder, the light on the mast and the cross-trees, the pelting rain and racing seas, the sense of confinement and the occasional slowly stalking ship, so powerful, so aloof, so unaware, made one of the strangest nights that I have ever had at sea. It was not until nearly daylight that we saw the first flashes of the buoys marking English Bank and by daylight we were up to one of them. The wind was down. We checked the number of the buoy and had breakfast beside it, then started the motor and headed for Buceo Yacht Harbour.

Once inside we found the water shoaling rapidly. All sorts of conflicting advice was shouted to us, to come here, to go there, to go farther up the harbour, to go back, and all the time *Tzu Hang*'s stern was unnaturally high and her wake clouded with mud. Eventually we were given the outer mooring where she settled comfortably on the mud and for the next three weeks was rarely fully afloat obeying neither wind nor tide, so that we could leave her without worrying whether the mooring was strong enough, or whether she would swing and touch some other yacht. She had completed the passage from Porto Praia to Montevideo in 39 days, having sailed 4,340 miles.

CHAPTER FIVE

Montevideo

Tzu Hang spent three weeks in Buceo Yacht Harbour and as
we were almost entirely occupied in getting her ready for the
Cape Horn passage we did not see nearly as much of Montevideo, or of its hinterland, as we would have liked.

One or two beautiful girls, dark-eyed sirens, relics of
Carronade's visit, appeared and tried to lure Bob away, and
seemed to me to shower him with untold promises of delight.
He remained like Odysseus, bound to the mast, up which he
discovered all sorts of horrors. We called him '*Los Ochos*' or
'The Eyes' and learned to dread his ascents and descents, or
indeed any time that he spent aloft where, like a monkey
searching its mate's fur for parasites, his eyes would become
riveted on, and his hands discover, some small crack or fissure
in the mast or its fittings.

'What's wrong now?' I'd call up to him.

'It looks as if the glue has gone here,' he'd reply, or 'there's
a hair-line crack in the steel here. It should be all right because
the fitting is bolted right through, but perhaps we should take
it off and have it welded.'

In the end we found that almost all of the stainless steel mast
fittings had a small crack somewhere or other, usually on the
old welds. We took them off and down to a machine shop in the
town, where a burly man, with a welding visor pushed up over
his head, took them from me, saying only, after a brief glance,
'*manyana a las onze*', and the next morning at eleven they were
ready. Worse than this was doubt about the glue in our new
mast. In places a line had begun to show through the paint and

54

when this was scraped it could be seen that there was a thin crack and that the glue appeared to have crystallized. We got a Lloyd's surveyor to look at this and he was most emphatic that we should have the mast banded or sheathed in glass-fibre before attempting the Horn.

Meanwhile, we took the broken staysail boom to the Yacht Club shipwright, a Spaniard who had emigrated from Riancho, in Muros Bay, near where we had been anchored a few weeks before. His spatulate fingers ran over the broken spar like a surgeon's over a broken limb, tender yet firm, so that we knew at once that he was a good carpenter. He was small and athletic with a bold look about his narrow brown face. The Yacht Club Uruguayo might lack something when compared with those stately Georgian buildings, standing alone amongst trees, above tall masts and white hulls, that one may find in the Solent or Oyster Bay, for it looked like a concrete YMCA, but it lacked nothing in its shipwright.

'See,' he said, 'it is nothing. I will put in a splice here. It will be ready tomorrow.'

His name was Martinez and we arranged for him to come on board to see if he could make us a low cover to fit over the sliding hatch, so that water could not force its way through the front and deluge the chart-table, as it was liable to do when going hard to windward. When he saw my drawing he quickly sketched a better design. 'No problem,' he said, and was back that evening to fit it.

'Come below,' said Beryl, 'and have a cup of coffee.'

He came below and his eyes ran over the interior, weighing and appraising. He did not approve of the unvarnished teak. 'It could be made to look very nice,' he said.

'Play him that song from Riancho,' I said to Beryl, thinking of the songs we had had at Punta Capitan. She put the spool on the tape recorder and suddenly the cabin was full of the harmony of Spanish voices and the notes of the guitar. I saw again the lovely Beatriz Recoy, so aristocratic and assured, the little, vivacious Christina Borras, and her two deep-voiced brothers, whose family had lived for generations at the farm

55

above the point. The cigarette smoke seemed to swirl again about the cabin, and the wine was on the table as they sang:

> '*La Virgen de Gaudalupe canto para Riancho*
> *La Virgen de Guadalupe canto para Riancho*
> *In todo Riancho ne hay una bella com ella*
> *Olinias venan, olinias venan, olinias venan e van*
> *No te embarke Riancho*
> *Que tu vas se mariar.*'

It is a nostalgic tune even for me and I looked at Martinez to see what effect it had on him. It had none. He had left Riancho without regret and was now hoping to leave Uruguay in search of better employment and better pay. 'What a silly song,' he said. 'Poor people. You know that they even pray to the Virgin for a better crop of apples. Tell me,' he said, changing the subject as Beryl switched off the recorder, 'would I be able to find work in Canada? I already have my papers for going there.'

'Yes, of course, any good carpenter can always get work at very good wages.'

'I am a very good carpenter,' he said, 'but my wife is happy here and doesn't want to leave, otherwise I would leave to-morrow. I think she would not find friends there and she only speaks Spanish. I can learn English but she cannot. It's no good here. I can't get on.'

We had not been at the Yacht Club long before we were asked to meet the Commodore and Flag Officers at a 'small ceremony'. We dressed up as best as we could and made our way to a small boardroom at the top of the building, where the Flag Officers, all immaculate in yacht club blazers and ties, were assembled. Commodore Hughes, a wealthy, urbane, and much-travelled man was at first a little taken aback to find Beryl with us, as he was unaware that the most important member of *Tzu Hang*'s crew was a woman.

We sat around exchanging pleasantries and bandying big names in a sort of social one-upmanship, until the Commodore floored us with an account of his visit to the Pope. Meanwhile we were being driven almost mad with hunger at the sight of most tantalizing cocktail snacks on the table, far superior to anything that we had tasted for weeks. Presently it was explained that we were only waiting for the champagne to cool. When it arrived the Flag Officers toasted success to *Tzu Hang*'s journey and we replied with a toast to the Yacht Club Uruguayo. After that the drinking and the eating became general and almost immediately the snacks were gone. Before leaving we were each presented with a club button, a burgee for *Tzu Hang*, and three small plastic models of life-belts inscribed in gold 'Yacht Club Uruguayo'. Three months later, when we found that it was necessary to have a life-belt for each member of the crew before we could be permitted to leave the Marquesas, I was able to assure the authorities that we had three life-belts on board.

Our next problem was the mast, which was solved by Captain Varela, who had recently commanded an Uruguayan destroyer, but was now retired and the local expert on glass fibre. We could not bring *Tzu Hang* alongside the Yacht Club wharf to take out her mast on account of her draught, but Captain Varela assured us that he could sheathe the mast as it stood. He did not realize the difficulty of the task he had undertaken until Bob and I hoisted him to the truck in the bosun's chair, together with his materials and a basin of resin resting on the top of a bucket attached to the chair.

He spoke to us in French, which we understood better than Spanish, and in which he was fluent. All the time he worked he talked and shouted at the top of his voice. 'It is absolutely impossible,' he cried, 'to work under these conditions. Impossible except for Varela. El Capitan de Fregate Varela. The expert Varela. See how well I do it. But what will my wife say when she finds me all covered in glass fibre. See I am the first man ever to put glass fibre on a mast like this, swaying in the wind. Always masts must be taken out and put on the ground on chocks. But this mast will never break now. I, Varela, promise you this.'

A piece of glass matting fell from the mast-head and drifted down to the sea. 'Attention,' he bellowed, making us all duck and wait as if a shell was arriving. 'Alas. My glass fibre. It has fallen into the sea. I am exhausted now. I must descend.'

Captain Varela was as wide as he was tall, but fortunately was of no great height. He found great difficulty in forcing himself into the bosun's chair. Between bouts of exhaustion and furious energy he came down for a mug of tea, the kettle being kept on the boil for him. During his numerous ascents he sat like a load of pig-iron, only putting out a hand to steady himself and never to assist by hauling. From time to time the bucket with the basin of resin caught under the cross-trees and down came a great dollop. Deck and halyards were soon covered in it and thousands of miles later traces still remain. As Bob and I hoisted what felt like Captain Varela and his frigate to the mast-head, our hair matted with glass fibre, we felt certain that no mast had ever been sheathed like this before, nor ever would be again.

'What do you think of Varela?' asked Martinez, when the job was done. 'Un charlatan—no es vero?'

He may have been a bit of a charlatan, but he made a good job of the mast. We felt no further worry about it and if any more deterioration appeared in the glue, at least we could not see it.

The disadvantage of the Yacht Club Uruguayo was that it lay far from the main shopping centre and the market so that we had to make almost daily excursions by taxi to the town. The steward of the Club, Antonio, was suave and helpful, a man of many interests. When we inadvertently transgressed by ordering bonded stores direct from the supplier and not through him he became cold towards us and we felt like the Hebrews when the Lord turned his face from them. Until then he was most helpful, disposing of our washing and providing his car as a taxi. The car was 40 years old and Antonio's brother who drove it was 70, and both of them were wheezers.

If we dared to open our eyes while being driven through the town by Antonio's brother, it was like stepping back 30 years in motoring history, for there is a high tax on imported cars. All kinds of vintage cars rumbled and popped down the narrow streets, their paint-work gleaming and their sacramental brass-work polished. Antonio's car, however, was only graced by age and on every trip to the town it began to smell as if it was on fire.

One morning we were visited by Señor George Ferier, an eminent eye surgeon and a keen yachtsman. Like all good eye surgeons he had an aristocratic, even a splendid, manner. He was a good-looking, tall man, well-read, enthusiastic and full of vitality. He was planning to buy a 28-foot plastic yacht in Miami and to sail her directly through the West Indies and along the north coast of South America, and then down the east coast to Montevideo, with a crew of five.

Bob and I, both appalled at the idea of so many people on so small a boat, tried to explain to him the difficulties of sailing a 28-foot light-displacement yacht for 2,000 miles along a difficult coast directly into the current and against head winds. It could only be done by motor-sailing, making use of the counter-currents and tides, and would require a very detailed knowledge of the coast and almost unlimited time. Few things are impossible but this approaches it, and we suggested that the only reasonable way was to take the circuitous route by Bermuda, the Azores, the Canaries and then to follow the course that *Tzu Hang* had taken, or at least a circle approximating to this route. Four or five men on a small yacht cannot make long voyages without putting in for water or supplies, so perhaps our suggested route, although long, was the best. The direct route has been sailed by the Uriburu brothers from Argentine in *Guacho*, but she is a very powerful ship with a big motor. They carried a lot of fuel on deck, motor-sailed most of the way until they were round the north-east corner of South America, and they were very experienced yachtsmen. It has also been sailed by *Ondine*, a very powerful racing machine, but I have heard of no one else who has done it. Mountaineers say that you cannot tell whether a climb will go until you put your nose on it and we have not done so, but I am certain that it is a very difficult passage.

Señor Ferier listened to us with about the same polite attention that he would pay to a patient protesting against the removal of an eye, but Bob was able to give him Bobby Uriburu's address, so perhaps he got some more experienced advice. Meanwhile, he arranged to take us out to see something of the country on the following Sunday.

We left on a gorgeous, sunlit day with all the traffic streaming out of Montevideo for the country and the beaches. The air was clear for there was not much industry and the view stretched to the hill tops or the horizon unless impeded by plantations of the dreary *pinus insignia* which is grown only to be gobbled up by the pulp mills, to make paper, 90% of which we could very well do without. Along the road were wire cattle-fences and on many of the posts a bird had built a mud nest, circular and about the size of a bowls wood, with a small aperture at the side.

The road led us back to the sea and eastwards along the coast to Punta del Este which we had passed on our way in and where expensive homes and luxury hotels are mostly occupied by visiting Argentinians. The wealth of Uruguay is more evenly divided amongst its population than that of Argentine and as a result the visitors from Argentine are apt to have larger yachts, longer cars, and more expensive houses than the Uruguayans. The Argentine money is appreciated, for Uruguay gives the impression of teetering on the brink of complete insolvency, the ultimate end of an over-socialized state. In Uruguay the working man has numerous holidays, guaranteed employment, an early pension, and free medical care with almost every other trapping of the welfare state that has been thought of so far. Even our cat had a tooth extracted at government expense! As a result of all this they have to keep a meatless day each week in order to preserve their beef for export.

We were often asked why we had come to Uruguay rather than Buenos Aires.

'Because I always heard how much the British Navy used to enjoy their visits here,' I replied, but in fact it was because it was less out of our way and also Beryl and I were registering our personal disapproval, to ourselves of course, of the Argentinian claim to the Falkland Islands which, at that period, had come again to the fore. In the books that we had on board I was able to learn something about the Islands. Although Hawkins had discovered them in the 16th century, nothing had been done about their occupation until Byron arrived in 1769. At Port Egmont in the West Falkland Islands Lord Byron planted a vegetable garden and took possession of them in the name of George III, unaware that nine months before Bourgainville had landed in the East Falklands and taken formal possession of them in the name of the King of France. The British did not establish a settlement until 1766 when Captain John McBride arrived at Port Egmont to carry out this task. In the same year he discovered the French settlement in Berkeley Sound and the two Governors were in dispute as to who had the right to be there. In 1767 Bourgainville delivered possession and the settlement to the Spanish, who thereupon turned the British out, but later restored the settlement under a secret agreement that it would be abandoned later. This was done in 1774 and brought the Falkland Island controversy to an end for the time being, but with the dissolution of the Spanish rule in America, the Falkland Islands came once more under the control of their original discoverers when, in 1833, we turned out a small settlement claimed by the Argentinians. Since then the British have ruled, settled, and developed them, and the Argentinian claim is as tenuous as a French claim might be to Louisiana or, for that matter, to Quebec.

From the expensive and artistic homes of Punta del Este we drove for miles along a country road, through range country of sparse grass and rocky outcrops, past rolling pampas and a straggling white-faced herd. We met three gauchos riding, wearing black sombreros and ponchos, a sheepskin under the saddle. They seemed far removed from socialism, but perhaps they had real and lasting wealth enough, a horse, a house, a wife, the pampas, and the arching sky. In places we could see the avenues of tall gum trees leading to the whitewashed buildings of scattered *estancias* and presently we turned back towards

Montevideo, stopping on the way to see the Union of Electrical Workers' Holiday Home, a country estate where the workers and their wives wandered in their best clothes amidst pines and playgrounds. We were checked in and out of the gate as if we were entering a secret installation, and the occupants of the car were examined to ensure that no women were wearing anything as disturbing as shorts. I felt as if I had come on a magic carpet to Russia. There are obvious advantages to such a holiday home, but one of them must surely be that the workers are eager to return to work at the end of their holiday.

We stopped also to see the factory which produces an excellent beer. Here, also, is a country estate, but one with a more liberal atmosphere, set amongst indigenous trees and gardens, and with plenty of opportunity for sampling the product, so that it has become a place of Sunday pilgrimage from Montevideo.

While *Tzu Hang* was in Montevideo, H.M.S. *Discovery*, on her way to the Antarctic, had called to pick up Lord Caradon, whom she was taking on a brief visit to the Falklands. We were invited to a cocktail party, given with the usual Navy know-how, and where most of the wealth and beauty of Montevideo were assembled. Her navigator and a tall midshipman were both keen yachtsmen, and arrived at the Buceo Yacht Harbour next day to visit *Tzu Hang*. The one carried a roll of plotting charts for us and the other was soon seated in the cockpit happily polishing brass. He was recently out of Dartmouth where he said the rule was: 'If it moves salute it; otherwise polish it'. Owing to the shrinking responsibilities of Empire, now almost gone, the Services as a career seem to be falling into disrepute, but I couldn't help thinking that anything that offers a trip to the Antarctic so early in a career, must still have a strong appeal for the young.

On H.M.S. *Discovery* we met Godfrey and Marie Cooper. Both had been in the Navy during the war. Godfrey had spent part of his time at the training establishment for frogmen and midget submariners, an instructor and a 'white rabbit' when skin diving was in its experimental stage. Marie had been a W.R.N.S. officer. The Navy puts its stamp on all its people, more than the Army, and although it was 23 years since they had left it, the traces were still visible, worn unostentatiously, a badge of pride. They lived in the tall Pan-Am building behind the Yacht Harbour and could look down on us from their window. They were always having us up for a bath or a meal, or calling to take us shopping.

On the afternoon of November 26th, we were ready to sail except for our fresh supplies. Montevideo was baking in sultry heat, waiting breathlessly for a *pampero* to clear the air. The water in the Yacht Harbour is never clean, but it was clean enough to tempt Bob that afternoon to plunge in over the side. His hands struck the soft mud and when he stood up the water was only waist deep. We began to wonder if we'd ever get *Tzu Hang* out even on the high tide next day, or whether she might not be destined to end her days like some of the other yachts around the harbour, which were gradually disappearing into the mud, with only a mast and slack shrouds sticking out of the water.

Next day Godfrey took Beryl off to collect the fresh supplies and when they got back he passed them and a bottle of champagne down from the wharf to the dinghy, 'to drink when you have got round Cape Horn', he explained.

'You don't seem to have very much there,' he added as he passed the last box down, but we were too busy balancing the dingy to explain that *Tzu Hang* was already carrying a vast amount of stores from England. When we arrived in Chile we had a letter from him. 'We were both amazed,' he wrote, 'that you could have made such a tremendous journey on that amount of stores. They would not have lasted Marie and I for a week.'

By 1630 the tide was high. We hoisted sail and started the motor. *Tzu Hang* began to move inch by inch at first until the fore-part of her keel came free from the mud, while the after-part was still ploughing in it. Then her head began to fall off and it looked as if we were bound for still shallower water. Gradually her pace quickened and she began to answer to the helm. Her bow came up and soon we were free and moving towards the breakwater heads. Godfrey and Marie were there to wave to us as we passed, and we set a course for the Buen Viaje buoy, and out across the River Plate, past the wreck buoy where the *Graf Spee* now hides her shame beneath the mud. Even her mast has vanished. The tall houses behind us soon disappeared and *Tzu Hang* leaned across the sea, reaching for the south.

CHAPTER SIX

Down towards the South

We were off. Every mountaineer must know the feeling as he starts on the climb. Gone were the tensions of preparation and planning, gone the quickening heart-beat as we read of gales and currents, great waves and battles against contrary winds. In two weeks' time we should be off Cape Horn itself. Gone were timid thoughts of seeking shelter. Like mountaineers, roped up and on the rock face, our thoughts were occupied in the immediate problems of the task, of how to overcome difficulties as they appeared, of making the best speed and of choosing the best route. We were isolated from the past and from the future and enjoying to the full the present moment, as if there was something added, an extra spice to life.

Tzu Hang felt good too. She was as good as she had ever been, and in her old familiar fashion she seemed to say, 'Let me go: give me my head.' We felt an unwarranted confidence and sometimes I referred to the future in terms of 'when we get round', rather than 'if we get round', only to see Bob and Beryl look at each other in mock horror at my over confident assumption that our future was not in the lap of Fate.

That first evening we sailed south along the western side of English Bank which lies blocking the River Plate off Montevideo, towards Cabo San Antonio, the south-eastern entrance point 80 miles away. Our fresh wind eased and the only interest during the night was to find a flashing light on the southern end of English Bank, which was not marked on our charts. By morning the wind was down and the sea calm. We motored for two hours with fog patches hanging about, which soon cleared off, burnt away by a blazing sun. A still summer's day with a hazy horizon, so that we never saw the coastline, but at about noon we saw an unmistakable *pampero* cloud moving up from the south-west.

It stretched for several miles, in fact right across the horizon in that direction. A long cotton-wool roll, dark below and greyish white above, and advancing steadily towards us. We had had all the warnings of a *pampero*, cobwebs in the rigging, hundreds of brown moths on board, and the sultry heat. As the cloud approached it took on a most alarming aspect, its top writhing like a wounded snake and spilling over its dark underparts. It was evil and menacing and, as it drew near, seemed to rush at us. We could see no white water under the cloud, but hurriedly clawed down all sail and awaited its passing under bare poles. The long cloud rolled over us, its darkness dissipating as it passed above the masts and it gave us only a derisive puff as it went away, as harmless as the smoke from a burning 'slash', that trails across a British Columbia sound.

Another was to come which had much more weight in it, soon after dark, and accompanied by torrential rain. This time of course we left it too late, and there was a sense of excitement and urgency as we pulled down the mizzen and rolled a deep reef in the main. The thunder crashed about us and the rain poured off the main boom at the tack of the sail in a solid spout of water, as if it was coming off the roof of a house. The lightning flashed repeatedly, brilliantly illuminating the glistening yellow oilskins and blackening the night in the pauses between. I looked aloft, as *Tzu Hang* heeled and hissed through the rain, and saw again the green glow of St Elmo's fire at the masthead, although not so bright this time as we had had it on our arrival.

At about three in the morning I awoke again to the sound of a rushing squall, and hurried aft to find Beryl with the mizzen already down. Again the lightning flooded the cockpit with sudden light, which made the compass glow. I could see her momentarily leaning over the boom as she tied the sail, one

66

foot on the tiller to prevent *Tzu Hang* coming up into the wind.

'Is she all right?' I called.

'Yes, I think so,' she shouted back. I was reluctant to come out into the rain, but put on oilskins and came on deck. A black cloud stretched low over us with the wind in the south-west. We were sailing fast towards the south-east. A safe course. I went below again and left Beryl to sit out her watch in the grumbling, rain-spattered night.

On November 29th we were 125 miles south of Montevideo, out of the River Plate now, the water no longer discoloured, and we tacked in towards the shore. During the morning *Tzu Hang* was making good time under her reefed main and jib, and as the wind continued to back towards the north we shook out the reef and set the mizzen. Early next morning the wind was light from the north as a fishing trawler overtook us from seaward, its lights all blazing, crossed the first orange glow of the sunrise and disappeared in the direction of Mar La Plata. It was a lovely morning, not a cloud in the sky, the horizon clear all round, and shipping passing up and down in shore. At about 1700 we could see the tall buildings and towers of Mar del Plata, when suddenly the wind dropped completely and then puffed sharply in the opposite direction, as if it had exhausted all its breath and had to take a sudden lungful, which caught *Tzu Hang* all aback. It was the last puff of the day. We started the engine and motored to the south in a calm sea. The lights of Mar del Plata glowed in the sky behind and the night was enlivened by the passage of ships on both sides, on their way up and down the coast. Next day the curve of the land in Rincon Bay had put the shore 200 miles to the west and we would not see it again until we approached Cabo Blanco 500 miles to the south-south-west.

It was December 1st and we passed a great concourse of sea-birds and supposed that this was the edge of the Falkland Current stretching up to the north, for the birds were screaming and diving and fish often seem to hang about the edge of a warm or cold current. The glass started to drop from its high 1020 mb and by evening *Tzu Hang* was running well under all sail and the starboard jib boomed out. Since Bob came on board we rarely used the twins, preferring to keep someone at the helm and the main set, rather than to allow *Tzu Hang* to sail more slowly by herself and put up with Bob's reproachful looks. By midnight the wind had freshened from the south-west and next morning we had 428 miles on the log and were sailing at six knots with a calm sea. We had several albatrosses and some large dark shearwaters with us. There are so many varieties that they are hard to distinguish, but these looked like the narrow-billed shearwaters, having a narrow grey bill. I have never had a suitable book for the recognition of sea-birds on board.

By evening the barometer was down to 1005 mb with high cirrus above us, and by midnight we had reefed the mizzen, which we later brought down altogether. There was a great deal of lightning about and then suddenly the wind disappeared, leaving an irregular sea in which *Tzu Hang* wallowed painfully. The engine was started but at daylight a wind from the south-east brought hundreds of moths on board, blown from the pampas and now being blown back. Few, I imagined, would reach it as we were now across El Rincon Bay, 100 miles from the nearest land. For weeks afterwards we found dead moths in shoes and drawers and bilges.

On December 4th it was a week since we had sailed and only 660 miles on the log at noon. We had used the engine for 21 hours in all since leaving Montevideo, as we were impatient to get on and were assured of plenty of wind farther south. In the afternoon, however, we did have plenty of it with the glass back at 1010 mb and at 1500 the wind switched to the south-east in a sudden cold squall, a refreshing promise of what was ahead. We were on the edge of the Falkland Current again, with any number of albatrosses, most of them with black backs, but a few of the larger wandering albatrosses were about, and innumerable shearwaters. In sunshine the squall whipped the tops off the waves, and a shoal of porpoises came rushing in to watch Bob and Beryl change the jib.

It was a brilliant scene of movement and stress as they

changed the sail—the wind blowing their wet hair and flapping their oilskins, the albatrosses swinging by so close that they could have almost touched a wing as they slid past the bow, the black squall cloud and the bright, contrasting sunlight, the white horses creaming towards us, and the porpoises riding their crests almost up to the side of the ship before diving beneath her, in such obvious interest and enjoyment.

When all was snug and we had taken in the log because a phalanx of porpoises continued to follow astern and sport with it, we all went below for tea, with *Tzu Hang*, her mizzen down, sailing well on the port tack. It was Bob's watch and he came down last, as soon as Beryl called to him that tea was ready.

Bob sat at the table with me and Beryl in the seat in the galley. She handed us mugs of tea, which we took in our hands so that it should not spill, but she put an open tin of chocolate biscuits on the table, which would stay there because of the rubber anti-skid net that covers it.

'Unrationed,' said Beryl, because the biscuits came from Uruguay and were not particularly good.

'Any ships?' I asked Bob, knowing that he would have had a look round before coming down.

'Nothing,' he replied.

It must have been hiding just behind the sail and had altered course to cross our bows for there was suddenly a deafening roar from above us that seemed to make the whole ship shudder. Down went the mugs of tea as we rushed for the hatch to find a huge tanker leaning over us, the stern just drawing clear, and the Captain waving cheerfully from the bridge, as he brought his ship back on to its course again.

'I do wish they wouldn't do that,' said Beryl, as we went shakily back to our tea, but from then on we passed no ship that did not come out of its way to inspect us. In fact we liked them to come, but not to catch us out like that. There is something very heart-warming and hospitable about a big ship that alters course to look at and to wave at a little one. It also gave us the feeling that at least we were not a commonplace occurrence.

During the next three days we made good progress. The water was shallow, between 40 and 50 fathoms, and pale blue in the sunlight. At times it was rough, with the wind one night blowing strongly from dead aft so that we seemed to be storming along in imminent danger of a jibe. On December 7th we got a distant sight of Cabo Deseado, just north of Cabo Blanco close to Port Desire, used by the early voyagers on their way south. Here came Byron in 1764 and this is what he said about these waters:

'Friday November 16. Shaped our course for Cape Blanco by the chart in Lord Anson's voyage. In the evening it came on to blow exceeding hard at SW x S, at 12 at night brought to under the mainsail and at daylight made sail again, there run a very great sea which broke very much. We imagined at noon we were not above 7 or 8 Leagues from the Cape. This may be called summer here but the weather is much worse than it is in the depth of winter in the Bay of Biscay. It is certainly the most disagreeable sailing in the world, forever blowing and that with such violence that nothing can withstand it, and the sea runs so high that it works and tears a ship to pieces. . . . At about 6 (November 17) we made the land bearing about S.S.W. which we took for Cape Blanco . . . it then began to blow harder than ever and continued so all night with a sea that broke over us continually and the ship worked and laboured very much. At 4 a.m. sounded 40 fathoms rocky ground. Wore ship and stood in again blowing all this time a storm of wind attended by hail and snow.' For the small ship voyager following the same course, Lord Byron's log is the best possible reading—after the voyage is safely over.

In *Ocean Passages for the World* the instructions given for the voyage south from Montevideo are as follows: '. . . if having called at Montevideo and bound to the southward after leaving or passing Rio de la Plata, keep well in with the coast. This can be done with safety as the winds are almost always from the westward, and an easterly gale never comes on without ample warning. Pass Cabo Corrientes at a distance of forty to fifty miles, and make the land to the southward of Cabo

Blanco and afterwards keep it topping on the horizon until the entrance of the Estrecho Magellanes be passed.'

That is what we had done and now planned to do, that is to say to keep the land topping on the horizon until we were off Cabo Virgenes at the entrance to the Straits of Magellan. We did not, however, see the land again, although I know that it would have been visible from our masthead, or at least the masthead of a full-rigged ship. This estimable volume goes on to say 'The older navigators, however, recommend that sailing ships [referring to the more direct route to Cape Horn] should keep within a hundred miles of this coast [the Patagonian] in order to avoid the heavy sea that is raised by westerly gales and to profit by the variableness of the inshore winds when from the westward.

'From October to March, when the sun has south declination, though the winds shift to the southward of west, and frequently blow hard, yet as it is a weather shore the seas go down immediately after the gale. The winds at this time are certainly against making quick progress, yet as they seldom remain fixed in one point, and frequently shift backwards and forwards six or eight points in as many hours, advantage may be taken of the changes to keep close to the coast.'

That, in a few paragraphs, was our bible for the trip south.

'What I want to know,' said Beryl, and she said it repeatedly, 'is what do they mean by ample warning? How are we going to know an easterly gale is on its way?'

The weather became colder and the glass now began to fall in earnest. There was something so relentless about its collapse that I felt sure a severe gale was coming, and gradually we eased our way in towards the shore.

On December 9th we crossed latitude 50°S about 50 miles off shore, so that we were well placed for a gale. By 1945 the barometer had dropped an inch from the previous morning, so that I wrote in the log, 'Since early yesterday morning glass has been dropping and now north wind has died out. Cumulus clouds are showing in SW. All indications point to a westerly gale. This is our first in these latitudes but assuredly not our last. I have an over-anxiety because we are in the south, but after a sleep this afternoon more relaxed—or resigned. Becalmed at tea-time and a jackass penguin braying to tell us what fools we are to be here. Motoring again as we are 40 miles off shore. 1945. Wind has come light and cold from the east. Under sail again.'

Unfortunately my log is rarely so introspective and I find it difficult to recapture the atmosphere of the time as I read it nine months later. The gale was reported as having blown at 125 m.p.h. and overturned 14 cars, removed various roofs, and killed 17 people on its way up the coast, where it created further havoc in Buenos Aires. Commodoro Rivadavia is a notoriously windy place and we were glad that our need to get south had prevented us from being off the Gulf of St Jorge when the storm struck.

On December 10th we were off Cabo Virgenes, at the entrance to the Straits of Magellan. Early in the morning a cold wind came from under a fog bank in the south, but soon the sun was up, the weather like a fresh winter's day in England, bright and vigorous. Later great clouds rolled out of the mouth of the Straits which they had been concealing and in the afternoon we waltzed round an elongated rain cloud that looked like the X-ray photograph of a leg. Our course was now 140°, and we were heading for the Straits of Le Maire. By now the glass had dropped to 982 mb but the weather was different and we no longer felt the menace of an imminent storm. A big tanker on its way to the Straits, coming across our bows, altered course to pass near us, and during the night I thought that I saw the light of an oil flare on the starboard quarter. When Magellan first came to these parts he called the southern part of the land Tierra del Fuego, because of the numerous fires that the natives kept burning ashore and in their canoes. Now the natives are gone but fires still burn along the coast of the Straits.

The next day again was clear and cold, with high cirrus spreading across the sky. We were accompanied by various types of albatross, giant petrels, diving petrels, sooty, manx, and narrow-billed shearwaters. The wind light from the south-east, or none at all so that we used the motor for eight hours, a swell from the north, and the glass giving no indication of rising. By the afternoon we had made sail on a course for the Straits of Le Maire and by evening the wind was freshening and the glass rising as the storm broke on Commodoro Rivadavia. Early in the morning we were hove to, but by breakfast were under sail again with the wind in the south west. A sunny day and a rough sea. By noon we had some glimpses of Staten Island about

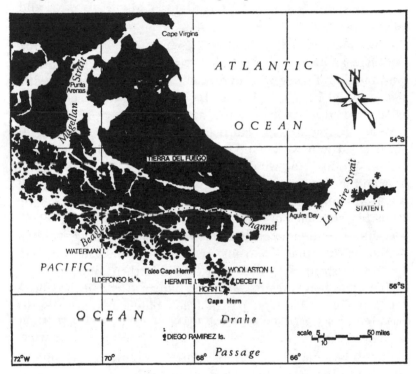

Cape Horn, Beagle Channel and Magellan Strait.

35 miles away, half-buried in cloud, and by the evening we were hove to 17 miles north of the mouth of the Straits in very rough water with the wind from the south and very poor visibility. There was no chance of getting through so we remained hove to for the night.

The wind blew at force 6 for most of the night, and by day-light was blowing force 7–8 but we were protected by our weather shore. Looking out of the hatch I spotted three mountains, but the wind or current soon put them out of sight. There was no trace of Staten Island, again buried in cloud.

With the wind in the south-west, but blowing south in the Le Maire Strait, we could have sailed for the eastern end of Staten Island. 'Oh, come on,' said Beryl, eager to get going. 'Let's give up the Straits and get on round Staten Island. We may wait for ever for a favourable wind. Let's leave the silly Straits.'

I was determined to hang on, so that we would not put ourselves another 60 miles down wind and down current, as we would do if we went round Staten Island. Bob agreed with me, so Beryl hadn't a chance. I picked up Moitessier's book which he had so kindly sent me, and read again the account of his passage round Cape Horn from the Pacific. Presently the wind eased and we got up sail, aiming to position ourselves for the Straits if the wind turned favourable. We were on our way and there was a feeling of adventure and excitement in the air. If we could make the Straits of Le Maire that night, it would be a big step on our way to the Horn. But it was Friday, December 13th, not a good day for the superstitious. I thought of the account that I had just read when Moitessier felt that he had the spirit of Al Hansen with him in the cabin:

'Tu as un bon bateau . . . un bon bateau . . .' said the spirit, 'et ta petite femme n'est pas mal non plus . . . mais n'essaie jamais dans l'autre sens . . . n'essai jamais . . . c'est trop dur . . . trop dur . . .'

It had become a joke with us. When things were uncomfortable we complained, 'Too hard, too hard.'

CHAPTER SEVEN

Cape Horn in the Early Days

The first ship to sail round Cape Horn was the *Eendracht*, which sailed in 1615 in company with a smaller vessel, the *Hoorn*, from the port of Hoorn in Holland. The two ships sailed under the command of the Shouten brothers and in the interest of a company promoted by Isaac Le Maire, with the object of competing with the Dutch East India Company by discovering an open ocean route westwards round the southern point of the South American continent to the Dutch East Indies, or to whatever else they might discover in the South Pacific.

The *Hoorn* was accidentally burnt in the bleak bay of Puerto Descado (Port Desire), on the Patagonian coast, while being careened in order that her crew might burn the weed off her bottom. The whole expedition continued south in the *Eendracht* and on January 20th, 1616, the ship was just south of the latitude of Cabo Virgenes, the Cape that marks the eastern entrance to the Straits of Magellan. They continued south and after three days sighted the north-east coast of Tierra del Fuego and on the same day discovered a wide passage between this and a mountainous land farther to the east. They were now exploring new waters and with what excitement they must have entered this Strait, wondering whether it was indeed the key to the route that they were seeking.

On January 25th, after being set close to the eastern shore, they scraped out of the channel and 'met with mighty waves rolling before the wind'. The wind was in the south-west, and the ship stood to the south-east, which was the best that she could do. On January 26th they were at 57°S and 'russelled mightily by a severe storm out of the south west'. The following day they wore ship and stood to the north. For two days they had been losing ground, but now the wind swung to the north-east and held there for two days, so that they were able to sail to the south-west until they had the prospect of two Islands 'set about with cliffs' which they named perhaps as a sop to the Dutch East India Company the 'Barnefeldt Islands', after its founder. On that same day they rounded the southernmost point of the land, an island whose southerly cape they called Cape Hoorn.

Soon after rounding the Horn the wind shifted and they were forced to the south again on the starboard tack and it was not until February 12th that they sighted Cabo Deseado at the western entrance to the Straits of Magellan. The *Eendracht* had sailed from the latitude of the eastern entrance to that of the western, by the ocean route round Cape Horn in 27 days, which would be considered not too bad a passage during the rest of the histories of sail and Cape Horn.

They sailed to the island of Juan Fernandez off the coast of Chile to rest and to recoup their crew, and from there across the Pacific to the Dutch East Indies where they were arrested and their ship confiscated by an angry Dutch admiral represent-ing the East India Company for having adventured too much too successfully. Of Isaac Le Maire's two sons who had sailed as supercargoes, one died on the way home with the Shoutens and his brother in disgrace in the Admiral's ship. In course of time the journals of the Shoutens and the supercargoes were read and given credence and so they were compensated for the loss of their ship and stores, while an official account of the voyage was made and distributed abroad.

This was the first passage round Cape Horn and through Drake's passage (for Drake had only seen it from the west and not sailed it), the forerunner of so many thousands to be made in the next 350 years, including recently that of *Tzu Hang*.

The publication of the report on the new route was received with great interest in Europe, and perhaps the most interested of all were the Spanish, who were particularly sensitive to any route, north or south, that might turn the flanks of their American empire. An expedition was ordered off immediately to check the truth of the Shoutens' story. It consisted of two caravels each of 80 tons burthen, under the command of Bartolome and Gonzalo de Nodal.

These caravels were fast, four-masted ships, square-rigged on the foremast and lateen-rigged on the other three. The Nodals came from Pontevedra and they sailed from the Tagus on September 27th, 1618, with a pressed crew of Portuguese sailors. They anchored in the Straits of Le Maire, in the bay of Buen Successo, on January 22nd, 1619, being the first to discover and make use of this bay, on the western side and almost through the Straits. Here they were storm-bound until January 26th when they set sail with a westerly wind south-east across the tide, but they were carried close to the south-west point of what is now known as Staten Island, which they named Cabo San Bartolome.

From there they tacked towards the Horn, keeping within the shelter of the coast of Tierra del Fuego and the offshore islands. Since Bartolome had a cape named for him, the next cape on the Tierra del Fuegan shore was called Cabo Gonzalo. On February 1st, when approaching the Horn, they met with a gale from the west and were driven back to Staten Island, and it was not until February 12th, having struggled all this time against westerly winds, that morning found them off Cape Horn. The wind was in the west-north-west and they steered south-west and found themselves at night close to two islands, which they named Diego Ramirez Islands, after the cartographer who accompanied them. One island was named Gonzalo and one Bartolome and the channel between them the Canal Nodales. They still had to fight strong winds and furious squalls and it was not until February 25th that they discovered Cabo Deseado ahead and entered the Straits of Magellan from the west. They passed through the Straits and returned to Spain.

Soon after their return, the Dutch equipped a fleet under Admiral Jaques Le Hermite, with the object of raiding the west coast of South America and continuing on to the Dutch East Indies. This fleet, known as the Nassau fleet, after struggling for some time to pass Cape Horn, discovered an island close west of it which was not on their charts, and which they named Isle Hermite, after the Admiral. They then came to anchor in the sound north of Cape Horn, which they called Nassau Bay.

During the first half of the 18th century the passages round Cape Horn were few and far between, and navigators on the whole preferred the better known and more sheltered Straits of Magellan. The Dutch had sent off another expedition under Hendrik Brouer, a few years after that of the Nassau fleet, and also with the object of raiding and harrying the west coast of Spanish South America, but they were not very successful, and returned the way they came. This expedition did not go through the Straits of Le Maire, but, being driven eastwards, found that Staten Land was an island and sailed south round its eastern point. Now, in 1721, they sent off another expedition of three ships under Captain Rogeveen, bent more peaceably on trade and discovery. They sailed through the Straits of Le Maire, one ship going as far south as 61°S and meeting with great icebergs. The ships were separated south of the Horn but made the island of Juan Fernandez, their rendezvous, and went on to discover Easter Island on their way to Batavia.

During all this time the British, although Drake had discovered the passage, had little to do with the development of the route, other than having a gunner on the *Eendracht* and by the passage of various buccaneers and privateers: such as Captain Bartholomew Sharpe in the *Welcome*, 1681; John Cooke with Dampier in the *Revenge*, which they had taken by piracy, in 1683; Dampier again, commanding the privateer *St George*, in 1703, and Woodes Rogers and Courtney with the privateers *Duke* and *Duchess* in 1708. England had first been too absorbed by wars and later too restricted by the Treaty of Utrecht, but in 1740 she was again at war with Spain and decided to send an expedition under Lord Anson, as the Dutch had done before, round Cape Horn to harry the Spanish trade and to attack their ships and colonies on the west coast of South America.

Anson's fleet consisted of the *Centurion*, the *Gloucester*, the *Severn*, the *Pearl*, the *Wager*, and the *Trial*, and with two fleet auxiliaries, the pinks, *Anna* and *Industry*, of which the latter was presently discharged. Anson arrived in the Straits of Le Maire on March 6th, but he was not out of the Straits before a westerly gale blew up, which nearly put H.M.S. *Trial* and *Anna* on the south-western point of Staten Island. From then on the whole fleet battled westerly winds until April 13th when, believing that they were 300 miles west of the most westerly part of Tierra del Fuego, they sailed north. Perhaps it was the Cape Horn current that they had misjudged, for when the low clouds lifted they found that they were close to a lee shore off Noir Island. Another gale blew them south and back round Cape Horn. The *Severn* and the *Pearl* gave up and sailed back to England, the *Centurion* and the *Trial* struggled on and reached the island of Juan Fernandez on May 28th and the *Gloucester* arrived on July 9th. The *Wager* was wrecked on an island, on the coast of Chile, which now bears her name. The pink, *Anna*, also separated from the fleet at the same time as the *Wager*, and on May 16th she was nearly driven ashore on the west coast of Chile in 47° 47′S latitude, near Inchin Island off the Chonos Archipelago. At the last moment an opening appeared in the rock on to which she was being driven and she escaped through it into a small bay which is now known as Bahia Anna Pink. From there, after two and a half months, her crew sailed to Juan Fernandez, arriving on August 16th; she was then unloaded and broken up in Cumberland Bay as it was considered she was unfit to sail to England.

Anson had sailed with the worst crews that ever left England, for they included 260 invalids from the Chelsea Hospital and a number of boys recruited for the marines. By the time the four remaining ships had arrived in Juan Fernandez, scurvy, exposure, old age, and other afflictions had reduced their strength from 977 to 351, but those who survived must have been brave and tough. In Juan Fernandez they recovered from their sickness and fortune turned towards them in favour.

As soon as the Seven Years' War was over the British gave their attention to the exploration of the Pacific. First came Byron in 1764. and since he had been a midshipman on the *Wager* and experienced the rigours of Anson's passage round Cape Horn, he was determined that the Straits of Magellan were the best way. Wallis and Carteret came next. Carteret had been with Byron in the *Dolphin* and no doubt Anson's journey was still fresh in the minds of both Captains. They, too, chose the Straits of Magellan, although the *Swallow* was an unhandy ship for the passage. In 1769 Captain James Cook with the *Endeavour*, on his first voyage to the South Seas, appreciated the protection that the islands would give until Cape Horn was rounded on the passage from the Atlantic to the Pacific and chose the way by the Straits of Le Maire. He was driven back out of the Straits on his first attempt, but next day made the bay of Buen Successo. He sailed from there on January 20th and doubled Cape Horn in fine weather keeping the land in view.

In contrast to the *Endeavour*'s passage the *Bounty*, under the command of Captain Bligh, failed to double the Cape and on April 22nd 1788 gave up the attempt and turned about for Table Bay. Between 1826 and 1836 the Fuegan Archipelago was chartered by H.M.S. *Beagle* and H.M.S. *Adventure*, but by now Cape Horn was becoming the great ocean highway to the Pacific. The early adventurers, however, had left their names, the names of their ships or their patron saints, like milestones along the route. Magellan gave his name to the Straits and Tierra del Fuego. The Shoutens named Staten Land, the Straits of Le Maire, the Barneveld Islands, and Cape Hoorn. The Nodals named Cabo San Diego, Cabo San Bartolome, the bay of Buen Successo, and the islands of Diego Ramirez, Admiral Le Hermite gave his name to Hermite Island, H.M.S. *Beagle* gave her name to the Beagle Channel, and, as survey ships are wont, named many other points and places, so these are the names with which *Tzu Hang* was to become familiar in the days ahead.

With the building of the Suez Canal and the sailing ship

casualties in the 1914–1918 war the era of the sailing ship was ended. Only Ericson and his fleet of grain ships were left to sail their easting down from Australia and round Cape Horn. Now they are gone and the only ocean-going sailing ships left are the training ships. Few of these, even the most modern with powerful auxiliary engines, can spare the time, while training cadets, to make a Cape Horn passage, except perhaps the Chilean training ship, *Esmeralda*. Cape Horn has lost its tall ships, a river of white sails that for 200 years flowed round it. For every seaman who passed it in all those years it was an adventure, something to boast about no matter how many times they made it, the fateful hinge of a voyage.

Cape Horn must feel lonely now, now that the sails have gone. But not entirely for it still remains as a challenge to yachtsmen who can find the time to go there. A challenge just as a high mountain is a challenge, for both can oppose those who essay to pass or climb them with bad weather, which may well bring disaster. Just as a mountain may be climbed by various routes, so Cape Horn may be passed in various ways, and the most difficult way is the ultimate challenge.

The easiest way to tackle Cape Horn is from the channels and islands and back into the channels and islands. As there is an anchorage on Cape Horn Island itself and numerous safe anchorages in the Hermite group, a voyage round Cape Horn need only be one of a few miles, and it need not necessarily be a difficult one. In fact during the summer the Chileans used to keep sheep on Cape Horn Island, which they brought to and from the shore in an open boat. All that is necessary to round Cape Horn in this manner is a good anchor, a good motor, and weather sense. I am full of admiration for the two single-handers, Bardiaux and Allcard, who made it like this, not only for their skill in handling their small yachts alone amongst the willywaws and currents of these islands, but for their courage and initiative in being there at all, but I do not feel that this is meeting the supreme challenge. As regards interest, their manner of doing it must far exceed the classic route and it is something that I should still like to do, for I love northern and southern waters and their shores and the wild-life that goes with them.

In order to meet the real challenge of Cape Horn a ship must sail the classic route from the Atlantic to the Pacific or from the Pacific to the Atlantic, passing the guardians of the Cape, the westerly gales that prevail in the area from southward of Cape Horn north-westward and northward off the coast of Chile as far as about 50°S. In that region, during winter and spring, between 30 and 40 % of all winds are force 7 or more, and in other seasons 30%. In all these regions at least half, and in the windiest part two-thirds, of these gales are force 8 or more. There are occasional periods in most years during which the wind blows with hurricane strength.

These are the daunting words of *The South America Pilot*. They mean that in any ten-day period in summer a ship may expect to meet three gales of which one may reasonably be force 7, one force 8, and one force 9, and if she is unlucky she may meet with one blowing force 10. Under these conditions it is surprising that there has not been more loss of life amongst yachtsmen who have attempted it.

Of the two passages round Cape Horn east to west or west to east, the old *South Pacific Sailing Directory* dismisses the passage from the Pacific as being 'so short and easy in all seasons as to need no comment', and *Ocean Passages for the World* calls it 'a comparatively easy matter, for the prevailing winds are favourable and the current sets strongly to the eastward as Cabo de Hornos itself is approached'. It gives December and January as the most suitable months.

But what may have been easy for a big square-rigger is not necessarily easy for a small yacht, and a gale that might send a big ship with only her topsails set, thundering on her way, might still endanger a small one and particularly a singlehander. Nevertheless, the keynote for a safe passage between 50°S and the Cape is speed, for the less time that is spent there the less likely a ship is to meet a severe gale, and once round the Cape she will have the protection, if necessary, from all winds from the north to the south-west, afforded by the islands. It was perhaps our mistake in our original attempt at Cape Horn that by choosing so southerly a route we were almost certain to meet, sooner or later, a severe gale. Would it have endangered a big ship? I have not the experience to say, but after sailing 130,000 miles in *Tzu Hang*, many of them in the higher latitudes, I know that it would have put any small ship in peril.

Like the north face of the Eiger, the supreme challenge for Cape Horn is the classic route from 50°S to 50°S, from the Atlantic to the Pacific. *The Southern Ocean Directory*, which so summarily dismisses the other, gives pages of advice on this route. It even considers the preference of sailing to ports on the Pacific coast of North and South America from the Atlantic by way of Australia. It is summarized in *Ocean Passages for the World*:

'The passage from east to west around Cabo de Hornos should usually be made in about 57°S, or at about 100 miles Southward of the Cape, but if after passing Isla de los Estados (Staten Island), the wind be westerly, the vessel should be kept on the starboard tack unless it veers to the southward of S.S.W., until in the latitude of 60° South, and then on the tack on which most westing may be made. On this parallel the wind is thought by some persons to prevail more from the eastward than any other quarter.'

The book gives the best time to make this passage as follows:

'June and July are the best months for making a passage to the westward round Cape Horn, as the wind is then often in the eastern quarter. The days are short however, and the weather cold. August and September are bad months, heavy gales with snow and ice occurring at about the time of the equinox. From October to March, the summer months, the gales are almost invariably westerly, in April and May slightly more favourable.'

The Southern Pacific Directory quotes verbatim the opinion of various Masters who have had wide experience of Cape Horn under sail. On timing one suggests that almost any time is preferable to 'the furious westerly gales of summer', while another says that having passed the Straits of Le Maire and profited from the weather shore that may be provided by the islands, and having arrived off Cape Horn, 'There is your enemy, and I say beat him if you can, and if you can't go round his flank. Go south to 60°S if necessary and try again from there.' As regards the Cape Horn current it seems to be the general opinion that it flows faster near the land, running as fast as two and a half knots between Cape Horn and Staten Island, but perhaps at only one knot farther south.

We had chosen our month, December, which is not recommended because of the constant westerly winds of summer, 'the furious westerly gales', because we felt that the summer winds blow at their hardest in January, February, and March, but above all because we knew that *Tzu Hang* was a good boat to windward and hove to well, so that we could risk head-winds in order to gain the long days and the warmer weather.

We had decided on the passage through the Straits of Le Maire because it provides better shelter than the passage round the eastern end of Staten Island, because it cuts out the worst of the current, and shortens the passage by 60 miles. But 'The conditions must be suitable,' warns *Ocean Passages for the World*. 'A vessel should not attempt the Strait except during daylight (for it is unlit) and with a fair wind and tide. The best time for beginning the passage through being at one hour after high water. A vessel should if necessary heave to off the entrance to the Strait until that moment. Under these conditions, even should the wind fail, or become adverse, a vessel would probably drive through rapidly for the tidal streams are strong. With a southerly wind however it would not be advisable to attempt the Strait for with a weather tide the sea is very turbulent, and might severely injure and endanger the safety of a small vessel and do much damage to a large one.'

It was these tide rips that drove Captain Cook back out of the Straits, almost exactly 200 years before, on his first attempt. Then 'The waves had exactly the appearance that they would have if they had broken over a ledge of rocks, and when the ship was in the torrent she frequently pitched so that her bowsprit was under water.' It is almost incredible that *Endeavour* could pitch so that her bowsprit was under water, as she had a high, bluff bow and her bowsprit cocked up at a steep angle.

Both Bardiaux and Allcard made the passage of the Straits singlehanded, Bardiaux being twice rolled over in the tide-rips. I am continually amazed at their hardihood. From Thetis Bay to Buen Successo Bay, and from there to Aguirre Bay are only short distances and the passages between them can be made in fine weather, but it is a harsh country and there is an aura of ill-omen about it, created by all the stories that have been told, some of them no doubt on the tall side, of bitter gales and escapes. If I remind myself that singlehanded crab fisher-men are facing the same sort of weather in winter in Alaska and the Aleutian Islands I remind myself also that they are not infrequently drowned.

The first yachtsmen to round Cape Horn from the Pacific to the Atlantic were George Blythe and Peter Arapis in *Pandora*, a 37-foot ketch of 14-foot beam. She was rolled over and lost her masts near the Falkland Islands, but had the good fortune to be found and towed in to Port Stanley by a whaler. Then came Conor O'Brien, writer and yachtsman, in *Saoirse*, which is still sailing now. Then Vito Dumas in *Legh II*, an Argentinian singlehander, who sailed round the world south of the three great Capes during the war, who has gained immortality on an Argentinian postage stamp, as well as with his dramatic writing. Next came the most silent and perhaps the ablest of all singlehanders to sail round the world south of the three great Capes, Bill Nance, making astounding passages in the 25-foot *Cardinal Vertue*. Then Moitessier and his wife Françoise in the 37-foot double-ender *Joshua*, in a great passage from Tahiti to Alicante. Then Sir Francis Chichester whose yacht, *Gypsy Moth IV*, also received the accolade of a postage stamp; a few days later he was followed by three young Australians, Andy Walls, Des Kearns, and Bob Nance in *Carronade*, whose passage was as secret as Sir Francis's was renowned. Then Sir Alec Rose in *Lively Lady* who, like Sir Francis, was a singlehander, so both captured the imagination of the British public.

Finally there came the survivors of the Singlehanded Round

the World race, Moitessier for the second time in *Joshua*, Robin Knox-Johnston, and Tetley in his failing trimaran, *Victress*. Ten yachts to have made the passage, and one that has made it twice.

Three yachts have rounded the Horn from the channels, or at least without facing the westerly gales south and west of the Cape, Bardiaux, Allcard, and *Stormvogel*, the famous ocean racer.

From the Atlantic to the Pacific on the classic route, only three have made it. First in 1932, was Al Hansen in his 36-foot Colin Archer, who sailed from Montevideo to Ancud in 101 days with his cat and his dog on board. Shortly after leaving Ancud he was lost at sea, and the wreck of his ship, *Mary Jane*, was discovered later on the coast of Chile, of all singlehanded passages perhaps his was the greatest. He made the passage in a heavy, old-fashioned ship with gaff rig and flax sails, the first singlehander to attempt it, but Al Hansen was drowned and the story never told. Then Warwick Tomkins in his pilot schooner *Wanderbird*, 85 foot overall and 77 foot on the waterline, which in 1936 made the passage from 50°S to 50°S in 28 days. A few months before *Tzu Hang* arrived in Montevideo an Australian, Tom Harrison, set off from the Falkland Islands to round Cape Horn, having sailed from Australia by the Cape of Good Hope to Montevideo. He has not been heard of since and it must be assumed that he is lost.

These, as far as I know, are the authentic passages. *Ahwanee*, the concrete yacht, so hard driven by Bob and Nancy Griffiths, did not actually go round Cape Horn, but through the channels after passing the Straits of Le Maire, nor did the great Slocum sail round Cape Horn, but was driven south after passing through the Straits of Magellan, until he escaped back into the Straits by entering the Cockburn Channel.

Of all the passages either way or any way, nothing can really compare with those made by singlehanders. When they are tired there is no one to take their watch, when they are anxious there is no one to relieve them of their anxiety, when they think they are sick there is no one to laugh them out of it, when they are fearful there is no one to lend them courage, when they are undetermined there is no one to harden their resolve, and when they are cold there is no one to hand them a warm drink.

Most recently came *Tzu Hang*, making the fastest east to west passage so far from 50°S to 50°S of 14 days, but for now she is just moving down the Straits of Le Maire. It is 1630 on Friday December 13th, 1968, the sky is overcast, the sea going down and the glass rising, and I have just seen again three mountains topping the southern horizon.

CHAPTER EIGHT

Tzu Hang *doubles the Horn*

The best that I could do in order to find our position in relation to the Straits was to take a horizontal sextant angle between the three hills, whose two outer summits were five miles apart, and the easternmost summit nine miles from Cabo San Diego, so that by laying off three times the distance I could ensure giving the worst tide-rips a good berth. It was towards this point that we now set our bow. We were making good time with the wind in the south-west, but the current against us. Beryl and Bob knew that I would be up and down all night like a cat on hot bricks, so they decided to share the watches, leaving me some time to sleep between the bouts of navigation fever that were already beginning to assail me.

Late in the evening in the long twilight of the high latitudes, I could make out what looked like a headland to starboard, but it was impossible to say whether it was Cabo San Diego, or the Terra del Fuegan hills behind the coast. By then we should have been about 12 miles from the entrance to the Straits and in another hour should have been able to see Cabo San Diego light. 'If it's lit,' said Bob gloomily, 'I shouldn't put any too much reliance on the lights, as they aren't very easy to service.'

An hour later I felt from my bunk that *Tzu Hang*'s motion had changed. I was fully dressed, wearing my oilskins and boots, and scrambled quickly aft to look through the hatch. Bob had freed the sheets and we were running through swirling tide-rips, while forward everything was blotted out by a long black rain squall which had just passed over. Bob was standing up as

88

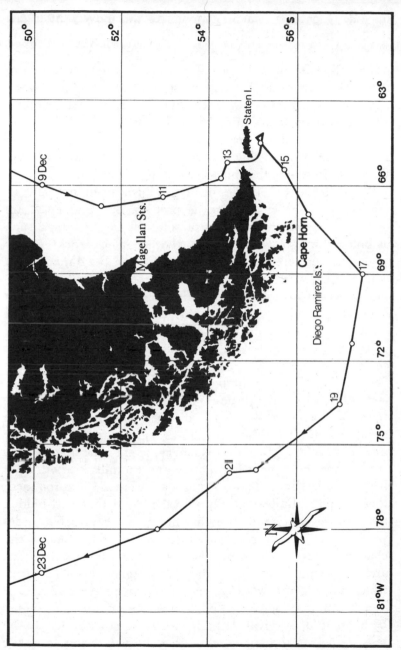

Doubling the Horn means sailing from 50° south latitude back to the same latitude in the other ocean—it took *Tzu Hang* 14 days.

he usually does on watch, swaying to the movement of the ship, his hand on the tiller behind his back, his eyes flitting continuously from compass to sail. His oilskin hood was up and he looked quite unperturbed. Suddenly I experienced one of those moments of doubts that must assail all navigators when approaching a pass or a coast, running fast, in poor visibility, when they have not definitely fixed their position. I began to wonder whether I had really seen Los Tres Hermanos, or had I made the mistake that other sailors had made and selected three hills in some other place to suit my expectations.

'We'll heave to,' I said, feeling faint-hearted but not altogether unwise. There were no protests. Bob and Beryl are quite capable of protesting in unison over minor things, such as going through a rocky channel when a less rocky one is available, but here I was on my own. Instead Beryl made me a cup of cocoa, which seemed to be the right treatment, and having recovered my nerve we continued on our way. About an hour later, Beryl who was on watch, called to me that she could see a light. It was about eight miles away, blinking irregularly as the black waves hid it, below an equally black cloud. It could only be San Diego light, whatever the interval of the flashes, and on the right bearing. With the tide now in our favour there seemed little doubt that we should soon be through. *Ocean Passages for the World*, my edition at any rate, says that the passage is unlit. Although various lights are listed in the *Admiralty List of Lights*, this was in fact the only one that we saw.

Soon the short night had passed and the hills on both sides began to take shape. Those to starboard were low and rounded, those to port climbed steeply into the cloud that had hidden them all yesterday and all night until now. At times both sides were concealed as a rain squall dragged over us. One of the characteristics of these waters is how quickly the wind will shift and a gale blow up, particularly in a channel such as this, which funnels the wind in one direction or the other. One moment all may be going well, and within minutes a ship may be fighting for survival. It happened to us now. Suddenly the sails slatted as the wind, which had been blowing from the

north down the Straits, shifted and blew up them. We hardened
in the sheets and looked anxiously to our heading. Behind us a
steamer appeared, her lights still burning, on the same course
that we had just followed.

'She must be the Argentine Navy supply ship, heading for
Ushaiaa, ' said Bob.

Sure enough she soon altered course making for the other
side of the Straits and, we supposed, for the Beagle Channel.
We also would have liked to have headed towards the western
shore, but now it looked as if we would have to fight to clear the
eastern.

It was my watch. As the long twilight gave place to day, I
could see from the passing coast not so far away to leeward,
what good time we were making. Sudden strong gusts came
ripping up towards us, making *Tzu Hang* heel and surge forward, but promising worse to come. As one followed the other
more and more quickly, she began to labour under too much
sail, pressing down into the water rather than sailing on it.
We were nearly out, but as the tide weakened, the current began
to set us towards the lee shore, and I saw that instead of passing
the coast we were beginning to close it, and to close it with
alarming rapidity. The bearing of Cabo San Bartolome, the
south-western point of Staten Island, was no longer changing.
It was the same point towards which the *Eendracht*, the ships of
the Nodals, and Anson's fleet had been set, and here were we
in the same predicament. If we were going to shorten sail before
something carried away we had better do it now, and quickly,
before we were too close to the Staten Island shore.

While Beryl pulled the storm jib out of the fore peak, Bob
brought down the jib. Trying to tame it singlehanded was like
roping a wild stallion. We could not run off to ease the task
as every yard that we saved might be of value. At any moment
I expected to see Bob take off, leaving the big sea boots that he
loved so well because of the extra socks that he could wear,
behind. Soon Beryl was up to help him and between them,
half obscured by spray, they set the storm jib. Then they rolled
another deep reef in the main and made their way aft hanging

on to the safety line rigged amidships from between the dog-house and mast, leaning against the heel of the ship, and the water cascading off their oilskins. Next we set the reefed mizzen and *Tzu Hang* was now in fighting trim, carrying all her sail but with a very small sail area. She went at the seas like a tiger, savaging them, hurling them aside with the spray volleying to leeward.

For some minutes the issue was in doubt and our only alterna-tive to put about and try to make Buen Successo Bay. While changing sail we had been set much closer to the cliffs and although still about two miles away, they were getting closer. Soon we could see the angry details of the breakers spouting at their feet, and the individual stones of the screes that lay in the gullies above them. Higher still the slopes of the mountains began to show under cloud, dusted with new snow. Beryl's eager face looked out from the hatch above the galley, where *Tzu Hang* was now trying to throw the eggs out of the frying pan. She was glowing from her recent wet struggle with the jib.

'How are we doing now?' she called.

I looked towards Cabo San Bartolome again and saw no change. I looked at Bob. He obviously saw no change. I looked again and to my relief saw a rock beginning to appear beyond the point of the cape.

'All right now—I think,' I called back to her, with more hope than assurance, but soon rocks, islets, a whole coastline began to unfurl beyond the cape. We were through, but with less than a mile to spare; little enough under these conditions.

By eight in the morning we were ten miles south of the southern entrance point but with the gale still blowing force 8 and a big sea rolling up from the south-west. We reefed the main right down and handed the jib so that *Tzu Hang* was hove to, then lashed the helm down. Like this she usually holds her position, making perhaps a little to weather and across the wind. With more sail and the jib aback she loses something to leeward. It is the most comfortable and the safest rig, so we all went below to catch up on our sleep. Four hours later I put up my head to find that we were 20 miles down the coast of

Staten Island in a current that must have been running at about four knots with the wind behind it. When the wind began to ease, a big sea still running, we set to work to try to recover lost ground, a third of what we had gained by the passage of the Straits, and slowly, very slowly the bearings of the hills began to change.

When Lord Anson's fleet passed through the Straits, they had a similar experience:

'We had scarcely reached the southern extremity of the Streights of Le Maire, when our flattering hopes were instantly lost in the apprehensions of immediate destruction: For before the sternmost ships of the squadron were clear of the Streights, the serenity of the sky was suddenly changed, and gave us all the pressages of an impending storm; and immediately the wind shifted to the southward and blew in such violent squalls, that we were obliged to hand our topsails and reef our main-sail: The tide too, which had hitherto favoured us, now turned against us, and drove us to the eastward with prodigious rapidity, so that we were in great anxiety for the *Wager* and the *Anna Pink*, the two sternmost vessels, fearing that they would be dashed to pieces against the shore of Statenland; nor were our apprehensions without foundation, for it was with the utmost difficulty that they escaped. And now the whole squadron, instead of pursuing their intended course to the S.W. were driven to the eastward by the united force of the storm and the currents; so that next day in the morning we found ourselves near seven leagues to the eastward, together with the force and constancy of the westerly winds, soon taught us to consider the doubling of Cape Horn as an enterprize, that might prove too mighty for our efforts. . . .'

We were still close-hauled soon after midnight when another ship appeared from the west, came up and passed close to us. She looked like a passenger vessel, a cruise-ship perhaps that had come down through the channels. These waters were getting positively crowded.

'She altered course soon after she passed us,' said Bob, who was on watch.

Slow 8' 25"   Dec 16ᵗʰ   19ᵗʰ day

0200 | Barnefeldt Gp bearing 303° - can just make nt Cape Horn South y Herschel. Glass is falling.   240 NW 4 1005

0800 76| Cape Horn bearing north about 5 miles - Sound between Herschel & Hermite is pr. The Horn is already half hidden under a curtain of misty rain. a bleak headland with bare bones of grey rock shining at it's top. The Islands rounded like the Hebrides - but many skerries & spikes y rock also. We have had a tide to help us out. Wind is backing so quickly as the glass falls that perhaps, perhaps, there is no great wind behind it. We are steering SW & can't say that we've doubled the Horn until we are on the other tack & have improved the latitude. Grey lazy sea, grey sky, rain, albatrosses gliding about, the only bright colours are Tzu Hang & one Fiskaris. Saw two of boats light - nt Barnevelds last night.

Pages from the log on the day *Tzu Hang* rounded Cape Horn to windward.

0900	Becalmed. started motor				2/4
11..	Fresh west wind - set			W	6
	storm jib and reefed				
	main & mizzen	205			
1330.135	Horn still in sight. -	205	W	5	1000
	set working jib.				
1430	Handed jib - set storm				
	jib - handed mizzen				
1500.	Blowing up force 7 # W.	280	W	7	1000
1700	Hove to.	200			
1930 801	Set storm jib & mizzen	205			
	Horrible toppling untidy sea.				
	Found luff wire of lost				
	storm jib was broken.				

'To go through the Straits?' I asked.

'No,' he answered, 'I'm afraid not. It looked as if she was turning up to round Staten Island.'

'Good God. Aren't we ever going to beat this current?' I started to think about heading south on the other tack, in search of more favourable winds and a lesser current, but before any decision was made the wind paused and then came lightly from the north-east. Soon the sea had calmed, and before it was full daylight we had the genoa up and were on our way directly towards Cape Horn.

It was December 15th, six days since we had crossed the 50th parallel, and hard to imagine that we were in the latitude of Cape Horn. We had our lunch on deck in oilskins and woollies, but warm in the sunshine, and drank a glass of Uruguayan wine. We were rested and refreshed and our smooth progress was marked by the passage of distant landmarks to the north, the bell-like mountain of Monte Campana near the entrance to Aguirre Bay, and the low outline of Isla Nueva marking the entrance to the Beagle Channel. Furthermore it was Sunday and we had two drinks to celebrate the end of a happy day. By then the wind had backed and freshened so that we were making about five knots. By 1800, as we drank our first drink, we sighted the Wollaston Islands, north of the Hermite or Cape Horn Islands, and about 30 miles away.

At midsummer in those latitudes, the twilight is never done, only its origin shifting from south-west to south-east, so that by 0200 we could see the Barnefeld Islands, two rocky ridges well known to old Cape Horners, sticking out of the sea about six miles away. Two small fishing craft, taking advantage of the good weather, were fishing just behind them. Deceit Island and Herschel Island were clear ahead, and a few miles beyond was Cape Horn, a small hazy outline, but I recognized it immediately as if I had seen it many times before. Here, where we had been expecting to fight for every yard, here we were, with genoa set, rippling along over a southerly swell, but an otherwise calm sea, as these ill-reputed islands, 'The uttermost parts of the earth', revealed themselves to our wondering eyes.

We felt as if we were trespassing in the halls of strange Gods, and that we must go past in silence, lest we awake their wrath. Bob was at the helm and I noticed a strange look in his eyes.

'What's the matter?' I asked.

'It's the enormity of it,' he said, and a jackass penguin popped its head out of the water not far away and brayed at us as we passed.

At 0800, Cape Horn was distant only five miles, a brown, treeless headland, with bare bones of granite showing near its turreted peak. It is not nearly so much of a horn as Die Hornung, the Horn of Iceland in the Denmark Strait, which is closer to the Arctic Circle than Cape Horn is to the Antarctic, and which *Tzu Hang* had rounded the year before, but because of its history it is infinitely more romantic. As I looked at it, although in southern latitudes, I thought of some old Viking sentinel, steel-helmeted and skin-clad, gazing moodily to the south. Not necessarily cruel for we had found it in a friendly moment, but hard. There is an atmosphere of *weldshmerz* about Cape Horn, of lonely hopelessness. Perhaps it is because there is no sign of human occupation, or perhaps it is because of all the pillared ships that once sailed by and now sail by no more.

If Cape Horn is to be seen only once, this is how it should be seen, with islands and dark sounds behind it, the very tip of that great continent. To see it in sunshine would be out of character; to see its dim outline through rain or snow, a triumphant sighting, still would not give it the impression of its being at the end of the habitable earth, as it had for us. No single ray of sunshine illuminated the drab slopes of its hills, no colour in all the dark seas around us, except for *Tzu Hang*'s red coat and the bright oilskins of her crew, so that even the slight yellow of an albatross's bill caught the eye. From False Cape Horn ahead to Deceit Island now behind, like the half-submerged backbone of some monstrous skeleton, all was clear, cold, and grey.

By nine o'clock we were becalmed while the albatrosses drifted past with only an occasional slow flap of their wings. It was not to be for long. 'There is your enemy,' the old sea captain had said, and sure enough the surface of the sea was soon ruffled by a puff of wind from the west. By ten o'clock we had set the reefed mizzen and storm jib and reefed the main to a strong west wind and Cape Horn behind us was already half hidden in rain. Our course was south-west on a heading that would take us well to the east of Diego Ramirez Islands so that we had nothing to worry about, and we expected to meet no ice unless we went as far as about 58°S, the probable mean limit of icebergs in December; but we were not in the least worried about ice, the only thing that we worried about was making good time and getting to the westward. Now the wind was backing so quickly as the glass fell that I hoped that there was no great weight of wind to come. By 1700 we were hove to, but an hour later were sailing again, still on a south-westerly course, with a horrible toppling sea that caught *Tzu Hang* at all angles.

December 17th came in with clearing skies and a rising glass as *Tzu Hang* struggled manfully along, still under very short sail, to the south-west. The squalls died down early in the morning and by 0800 we were under reefed main, full mizzen and working jib. We were soon back to reefed mizzen and storm jib and continued so all day, taking advantage of every swing of the wind to improve our westing. In the evening the wind suddenly died altogether, as if it had said, 'All right. You can take a break,' and we ran the motor for a short time, with the mainsail set, to charge our batteries and steady *Tzu Hang* against the uncomfortable sea that the wind had left, but within an hour it was back again and this time from the north. We had reached our farthest south, latitude 57° 45', for all next day the wind stayed in the north. That was a splendid day. It was a variable wind, keeping us busy all the time with sail changes and sometimes swinging so quickly that we had to change our tack. As busy as if we were racing, which indeed we were, racing to make our westing while we could. At ten o'clock that night, with the wind slightly east of north and a much steadier sea, we were making five knots to the north-west and 120 miles off the coast. We 'thanked with deep thanksgiving whatever gods there be' that were looking after *Tzu Hang* and sending her so splendidly on her way. A few miles now and we would be round the corner. The wind could blow from the west—although better from the south-west—and we would be able to hold our course.

December 20th was another splendid day, when between noon and noon of the previous day we made 155 miles to the north-west, at times with all sail and the genoa set, but by nine in the morning we were back under short sail. The glass was falling fast and by midday the wind was again in the west and there was every sign of an approaching gale. After our two previous experiences I could hardly describe myself as awaiting its outcome with equanimity, but rather one of anxious wondering just how far the glass was going to fall, and how long the gale would last. We went through the well-known process of increasing the reefs and reducing the sails until all we had left was the main, rolled right down to the reefing eyes, the head of the sail well below the upper crosstrees. It was a strong new mainsail, now the size of a small trysail, and *Tzu Hang* was hove to on the port tack. She kept four to five points off the wind, climbing up the face of the waves and ducking quickly over their crests, with only an occasional splash of spray on the deck. We were 130 miles off the entrance to the Cockburn Channel into which Slocum had escaped, when driven south from the western end of the Straits of Magellan. As *Tzu Hang*'s drift appeared to be due north it looked as if we were in no danger of having to follow his example.

However anxiously I might put my head out of the hatch, to judge the wind strength or turn to study the glass to see how much farther it had fallen, Beryl, since it was difficult enough to sleep, decided to employ her time more usefully. She and Bob were soon deep in a discussion about bread-making.

The folding oven was assembled and wired on to the stove, and the bread was mixed and put in the head, together with various oil lamps in order to achieve the right temperature, so that it would rise correctly. Oblivious to the rising wind and the threatening grumble of breaking crests, miraculously stable in the reeling instability of the cabin, like two alchemists bending together over pans and stove, they managed two bakings which took half the night and ended with eight fresh brown loaves slung in a netting hammock under the deck-head. While I tried to sleep the cabin was filled with the homely smell of the bakery and earnest talk about bread, a mystic communion, punctuated from time to time by triumphant exclamations of, 'Coming up nicely', and 'Beautifully done', and once on a more doubtful note, 'Give it a bash on the bottom and see if it comes out'.

No gale can stand up to this sort of thing and by midnight the glass had steadied and it looked as if we had seen the worst. Since 1500 it had been blowing force 9, with perhaps some stronger gusts. Now that the cooking was over I lay listening to the song of the shrouds, a deep note that rose to a higher pitch as *Tzu Hang* rolled towards the wind. '*Tzu Hang*, hold hard—hold hard', they seemed to say and she was doing it easily enough. No water had splashed on to the deck for some time, and there was a new note in the shrouds. 'You may go— you may go', they were singing now. The glass had moved up and when I looked out I found that *Tzu Hang* was facing more directly into the sea as the wind shifted to the south-west. There was a big sea running and I thought it better to wait a little longer before we got going.

We set sail again after an early breakfast, setting at first only the storm jib in addition to the reefed main. *Tzu Hang* was soon flying along the run of the sea, so that she was side-ways to the crests as they came racing up. Although we were boarded once or twice by a wet one, which brought a shout of disgust from the helmsman cowering under the canvas dodger and heeled *Tzu Hang* far over, there was no danger in them now. We were fairly footing it to the north-west, piling up the miles across a grey and deeply furrowed sea, the grey clouds hurrying low above us. They gave us a chance to get a glimpse of the sun's dim outline and we found that *Tzu Hang* had held her position well during the night and by noon next day we had made another 155 miles to the north-west and were 100 miles west of Los Evangelistas light, at the entrance to the Straits of Magellan. On both of these days we had had hundreds of

little grey and white Antarctic petrels sporting round us, but
as we crossed the latitude of the Straits they disappeared and
we saw no more of them. Perhaps we had reached the edge of
their district, or perhaps it was just time for dinner and the food
was elsewhere, but anyway they were gone.

On the 22nd we were still making splendid time, the barometer rising fast and the genoa set in the afternoon. We had
Commerson's dolphins with us again, their white noses and black
saddles showing clearly as they dived across our bow. Venus
showed two hours before sunset, close to the moon and looked
like *Apollo 11* on its way. We wished the astronauts our kind of
luck. Next morning, December 23rd, we crossed the fiftieth
parallel again, and were able to alter to a more northerly
course. *Tzu Hang* had doubled the Horn in 14 days without
the loss of a shackle pin. It would be considered a good passage
for a fast square-rigger let alone a 20-ton yacht, so that we were
very happy. We were not through the forties and we were not
going to feel absolutely secure until we were passed them, but
coming from the fifties into the forties is like coming into a new
climate altogether. We could not believe that there was any
great danger ahead. Also we had been there before. It was
almost like coming into home waters.

Carteret, on clearing Cap Pillar and arriving at approxi-
mately the same position as we were now in, wrote in his journal,
'Being now in high spirits and hoping that in a short time we
should be in a more temperate climate.' It was the same with
us. Carteret's hopes were soon disappointed. The account of
Lord Anson's passage, 'of high winds, foul weather and tur
bulent seas, might with great propriety serve to describe
what then happened to me', he writes, but on the other hand
Commodore Byron on arriving in this area found, like *Tzu
Hang*, little worse than a 'prodigious great western swell'.

CHAPTER NINE

To meet old Friends

For the time being our luck stayed with us and we sailed out of the 'low' that had sent us so wonderfully on our way, and into the bottom of a 'high', so that we kept the west wind. Gradually it weakened and shifted to the north, bringing a grey drizzle, until it dropped altogether, and we spent all one night and most of next day under power.

All day the grey clouds loitered above us, and rain squalls came drifting up towards us in an indeterminate way, always receding before they passed over us, as if they had wandered up to satisfy an idle curiosity only, and leaving without even a puff of greeting. All day the albatrosses came sliding miraculously over the dark unruffled swell, only deigning to give an occasional flap of the long end section of their wings. All day Bob watched the horizon hoping for some portent of wind to come. It came in the evening unheralded from the south, and since it was Christmas Eve we set the twins, and settled down to the most relaxed night since we had left Lymington. We listened to carols from far away, as *Tzu Hang* rolled her way to the north, and thought of the many Christmases that we had spent on board or near her, for the past 13 years, never in the same place. That night, when Bob turned into his bunk, we hung a woollen sock full of small gifts topped with a traditional orange outside, and then solemnly hung similar socks above our own bunks. The coming of Christmas day was marked by a carol of porpoises, all dressed in green phosphorescence, drawing bright lines about *Tzu Hang*'s bow, and as daylight came the albatrosses, cape pigeons,

NATIONAL AERONAUTICS AND SPACE ADMINISTRATION
MANNED SPACECRAFT CENTER
HOUSTON, TEXAS   77058

IN REPLY REFER TO: AP7-1892   June 25, 1969

Brigadier Miles Smeeton
Canadian Imperial Bank of Commerce
Pender and Howe Street
Vancouver, Canada

Dear Brigadier Smeeton:

Colonel Borman has asked us to send the enclosed photographs to you, in
hopes that they will fulfill the requirements of your letter of June 13.

It is most interesting to learn that, while Colonel Borman and his two
companions were alone in the far reaches of the ocean of space, you and
two companions were also alone in what, when all is said and done, is
probably a more deadly sea.

Please let us know if we can assist you further.

                              Sincerely,

                              Carl R. Hart

                              Carl R. Hart, Chief,
                              Broadcasting Services Office

Enclosures

This generous letter was sent by NASA after I had written to Colonel Borman
asking if I could get a copy of the photo of a storm approaching Cape Horn that he
had reported from *Apollo 8*. His photo showed this effectively.

shearwaters and petrels seemed to welcome and escort her. We still had the same grey sky, but the Christmas present of a fair wind held all day, and we ended it as other people were doing in many parts of the world, with a sensation of having eaten too much.

On Boxing Day the wind dropped in the morning, but at about ten o'clock it was back again, the glass falling and squalls blowing in from the north. It was the anniversary of our second capsize and we were not so far away from the position at which it had occurred. The wind was blowing exactly from the direction in which we wished to go and I neither wanted to close the coast, nor to sail farther west, so we compromised by heaving to for the night. On the 27th and 28th the wind was still from the north, so that we were forced to submit and steadily closed the coast of Chile until we tacked and sailed offshore. That night we were becalmed well north of the position where *Tzu Hang* had found the blessing of the south wind, as she stumbled back in her crippled state eleven years before, perplexed by the same northerly winds that were harassing us now.

In the morning the long unruffled swell came rolling in from the west and rolled on to the east, the only wind being caused by the lift of its passing. Only the albatrosses could make use of it, and sometimes we could see just the tip of a wing sliding along the top of a wave with the rest of the bird concealed behind it. From time to time they would land near the ship, thrusting their feet out to skitter along the water as they came down, and then going through the elaborate process of folding their wings section by section until a final shuffle put them neatly in place.

We had finished our fuel and felt that we might be becalmed for days. We filled in the time by changing the 'Cape Horn mainsail' for an older and lighter one. As we hoisted the sail, oiling the slides, and checking that all was well with it, the painted swell to the south suddenly appeared crinkled in patches, and a moment later a breath of wind fanned our cheeks. We dared not believe that this was the south wind at last. We had been in despair about our fast passage being ruined, hardly speaking to each other, but now, as the sail filled, all was gay again. We boomed out the headsail on the other side from the main, and all day the wind freshened over a blue sea sending the little waves trickling past. With the wind came a new shearwater, the New Zealand shearwater which nests on the islands of the Chilean coast, and looks as if its eye has been touched with mascara, like the fork-tailed petrel that we had got to know so well in the Bering Sea. Soon the sea began to put on its gala ribbons and rosettes, as the little shearwaters swooped and swung about us.

On December 31st we continued to sail exultantly north-wards, with the seas now piling up behind, and *Tzu Hang* in her glory. At midnight we all assembled to drink the bottle of champagne that had been given us in Montevideo.

'Point it out of the hatch,' said Beryl, 'and mind the cat.'

'Here it comes,' said Bob, holding his glass ready.

I worked away at the cork with my thumb. It seemed to be a tight-fitting cork. Suddenly it toppled over and fell to the ground. The champagne was absolutely flat and tasted of raisins, but it was not symbolic of our spirits nor of our sailing, for we were foaming along.

Next day, after passing a steamer heading south and inshore, we made La Mocha Island our landfall, the landfall that Drake had made on his passage north from the Straits and where he had stopped to take on water and had lost two men, killed by the natives, whom he supposed had mistaken them for the Spanish. It was the landfall that *Tzu Hang* had also made when she first approached this coast, when its northern edge had appeared, a thin hair-line against the grey distance. Now the whole island seemed to spring suddenly large and near from the Chilean coastal haze that had concealed it. We passed it at about eight miles wishing only to complete this part of our journey without mishap and as soon as possible.

Early next morning I sighted the brown cliffs of Punta Lavapie, with Santa Maria Island beyond, guarding the entrance to Coronel Bay, the island that *Tzu Hang* had once crept past without a rudder and in fog, in search of shelter.

This time we had no need of shelter. Here *Tzu Hang* came proudly, storming along, tossing a white ribbon behind her, shaking her head at the shoals that eleven years ago, if the gods had not been on her side, might so easily have embraced her. Now there ahead were the three points of the Bio Bio hills, one of which we had climbed, and there the Pan D'Azucar, the grey rock below the house at Tumbez, where we had stayed. Here at last was Tumbez Point, and in came the sails close-hauled as we rounded it to tack up the Boca Chica.

We sailed up in fierce hard tacks, for the channel is narrow and the wind was blowing freshly straight down it, tacking in towards Lo Alfaro, Admiral Young's house on the shores of the sound and flying a signal, 'Compliments to the Admiral'. It was Admiral Young who had helped us so much during our previous stay, and it was from here that he and his daughter, Cecilia, had put off in their small boat to wish us luck as we left. So we tacked on, remembering the landmarks and pointing them out in excitement to Bob, until we came to the anchorage near the Navy Base. Our moment was over. The chain rattled out and *Tzu Hang* was still, her wings folded. It was as if she was suddenly humble, she and her crew. As if she and her crew wished to say thank you, to the winds and the weather and whatever there is, for a good passage, and to the country that now sheltered us again, for her care.

We sat listening to the welcome sounds of the shore, as every seaman does after a long passage, thinking of our mail and of how soon we could get it. From this distance the shore looked clean and inviting. It is hard after a passage to realize that all is not necessarily good ashore, that one may soon be short-changed, robbed or run over, that one may lose a ticket or catch 'flu. It takes a few days to recover the protective shell necessary for survival in civilization. For the time being, until the Port Doctor arrives and gives pratique, and the yellow flag comes down, there is the pleasant anticipation of going ashore soon. For the time being it is sufficient to have arrived.

First came the Port Captain, who was brought out by an agent of one of the shipping lines in his launch. We went below and soon the drinks were out while we tried to catch up on old friends.

'Where is the Admiral?'

'The Admiral is here. He is very well and has not changed at all.'

'And Mrs Young and Cecilia?'

'Both are well. Nothing has changed.'

'And Edward Cooper?'

'He is the same. Nothing changes here.'

'Does he still live in Concepcion, and does he still have the same house, and the three maids, Carmen, Lydia, and Theresa?'

'It is all exactly the same, only they are older. The youngest maid has had a baby. By the gardener it is said. Of course we have had a big earthquake, that is all that is new.'

'And Commander Porter?'

'Oh. He is the big noise now. He is the Commander-in-Chief.'

The Port Captain was a Naval officer with polished manners, who spoke English well and lived with his family in a flat over the office.

'You are not supposed to anchor here,' he said now, 'so if you do not mind we will move you into the fishing-boat harbour. It will be right under my office so that we can keep an eye on your ship for you when you go ashore. Shall we tow you?'

We had kept sufficient fuel for manœuvring in port, so I told him that we would follow if he would guide us.

'I'm sorry that you will not be able to go ashore until the Port Doctor has been on board,' said the Port Captain as he left, and the agent added under his breath, 'Be careful of the Doctor. He is a bad man.'

'I suppose he must have had a brush with him over some quarantine regulations,' suggested Beryl, after they had gone.

The Port Doctor certainly took his time about coming. At about eleven next morning I hoisted the signal to say that a doctor was required on board. He turned up soon after although I do not expect that my signal had anything to do with it, and after a few questions gave us pratique. There seemed to be nothing bad about him. The Customs Officer came with him and we were soon cleared.

I rowed Beryl ashore so that she could telephone Edward Cooper, and while I was beaching the dinghy, heard a soft voice behind me, saying:

'Hello, Miles. So you made it all right this time.'

I turned round to find the Admiral standing behind me and, as I had already been told, hardly changed in eleven years. Still the same slight and erect figure, and the same quiet manner, wearing his hat, his tweed coat, and his grey flannel trousers like a uniform. I was so pleased to see him.

'Hello, Admiral,' I said. 'How are you? Did you not see Beryl? She has just gone ashore to telephone Edward. Yes, we did. From 50°S to 50°S in 14 days.'

'Well done,' he said. 'That is very good going. Especially for so small a ship.'

He knew well what he was talking about, for he had taken the Chilean training vessel, the three-masted ship that they had before the four-masted barquentine *Esmeralda*, twice round Cape Horn.

'How do you like her colour?' I asked.

'It suits her very well. She looks in fine shape. You know your book that you sent me? Well you remember how you always made me say "Not true?" at the end of every sentence, like "*No es vero?*" Well I've never said it since.'

'Oh, Admiral. I am sorry.'

He laughed. 'You know,' he said, 'I lent that book to someone and I have never seen it since. You must get me another.' I waited for the 'Not true?' but I never heard him say it again.

The eleven years of our life, since we had left Chile, had been so full of incident and adventure that it felt almost as if we had crammed a whole lifetime into them. It was almost impossible to believe that there could have been so little change here. It was like opening an old trunk in the attic and finding all sorts of treasures, long since stowed away and forgotten. We found ourselves picking up the threads of a conversation as if it had been dropped only a week ago.

Edward arrived to take us up to Concepcion, to the house where we had stayed with him so long, to the luxury of long hot baths, and in one of them a remembered stain in the enamel, a little larger now.

'Edward,' we cried, as he stepped out of the car, 'you've got a new car.'

'Well, yes,' he said. 'Do you remember the old one? It was rather on its last legs when you were here.'

The house was just the same, secretive behind a high wall, almost on the edge of Concepcion, overlooking the river. Sweet madonna-faced Carmen, an old lady now, arms folded across a white apron, hands holding the elbows, and kind Lydia, the lame cook, and Theresa the young mother, looking most unlike a madonna, were lined up to receive us. The cat was taken away immediately to the kitchen to be fed and petted. Almost at once she jumped up to the small high window which she used to use as an exit to the garden, but which is now sealed. She remembered everything as clearly as we did. Edward had inherited his maids and was now landed with them, the servant of his servants, working all day in the office to keep them in the circumstances that they were accustomed to, a man so gentle that he would be unwilling to make any upheaval that would cause them distress.

We had to inspect the new baby, a monstrous child, the newest cuckoo in the nest. 'He's called Edouardito,' Edward told us with a coy giggle, and added needlessly that he had had nothing to do with it. 'Actually he's called Edouardito Harry, which lets me half out. You remember Harry Price who lives just down the road?'

Unfortunately the gardener, the father, refused to marry the girl, so Edward, *in loco parentis*, and not being a shot-gun man, had had to sack him. As a result the shrubs and bushes that filled the garden were daily growing larger, like the child, and the spaces smaller. It was one of the few changes that we noticed, that and some new blocks of flats on the road to Concepcion and a new bridge over the river.

There used to be a large English colony in Chile, whose

children, like Edward, went to school in England and later fought for England in the war and maintained their English nationality and national characteristics with pride, as did the English in Argentine and Uruguay. Now all this is changing. Money does not come so easily and the expenses of an English education are high. English children are either educated in Chile and become Chileans, or the families leave for employment in England, Australia, or Canada, so that their children may remain British and be educated in an English-speaking land. Gradually the English are disappearing, leaving people like Edward, who have the '*padron*'s' feeling of commitment towards their employees, out on a limb.

'You must come to Canada,' Beryl told him, 'and stay with us like we stayed with you, for at least a year. We would play golf or take prodigious walks again.'

'Well if things go on like they are doing now, what with business falling off and inflation and this socialism, it may come to that,' he said.

'You talk about business being so bad and the economy on the point of collapse, but really I think things look better than when we were here last,' said Beryl. 'The trenches are filled in in the streets in Talcahuano, the roads are better, you have a new bridge, and there are those new buildings on the road into Concepcion.'

'It's not really a very impressive list, you know,' he replied, 'and of course we've had our earthquake. The whole economy of Chile depends on having a bad earthquake every 40 years. It has to be bad because then money pours in from outside in earthquake relief funds, and the Chileans respond to an emergency and work hard to put things right. It must not be too frequent otherwise it would lose its novelty and we wouldn't get the same response. That's how we get our new buildings and bridges.'

'One thing about Chilean servants,' said Beryl later, still worrying about Edward, 'if the worst came to the worst and there is a complete economic collapse Edward's servants would always look after him, although perhaps not quite in the style

to which he is accustomed. We just have to get him married,'
she added. Every woman who has ever met Edward is determined to get him married. It presents the same challenge
as sailing round Cape Horn.

One of the characteristics of the harbour at Talcahuano is the
train that still shuffles round its perimeter to the dockyard and
Naval base, and one of the characteristics of the train is the
black smoke that volleys from the engine and spreads out over
the harbour, and while we were there on to our sails. When
Captain Horn of the Chilean Navy invited us to move to the
anchorage off the Navy Training School on Quiriquina Island
and sent us a tall Lieutenant to pilot us, we were glad to go.
He stepped off the iron rail of the large Quiriquina ferry on to
Tzu Hang's side, sending Bob and I flying in search of unneeded
fenders, horrified at the speed of its approach, and unaware of
the Captain's judgement. Everything done by the Chilean Navy
has a certain *élan* about it.

At Quiriquina we anchored off the end of a long pier in clear
water but we felt that we could not take advantage of the
hospitality of our friends much longer; they were the only
excuse that we had for staying, for Beryl had stocked up with
stores and *Tzu Hang* was ready to go. We were short of charts
and pilot books because we had hoped to get them for our on-
ward journey to the Marquesas and Hawaii in Talcahuano,
but they were not available. A Navy captain gave me a chart
of Juan Fernandez and San Felix Islands, but for the rest we
had to rely on a page of the chart catalogue. This at least
showed the position of the islands accurately and the early
discoverers were not nearly so well informed. The page from
the chart catalogue, a new cockpit floor and some welding done
to a spinnaker boom were all the gifts of the University Yacht
Club in Talcahuano. We sailed from Quiriquina Island across
the Boca Chica to Lo Alfaro, the Admiral's house. His grand-
son, a naval cadet, and two small grandchildren had laid a
buoy for us, marked with a flag, at the spot at which we were to
anchor.

However gloomy the future might appear in Edward's or

the Admiral's eyes, they lived extremely well in the present. The sun shone, the gardens gave liberally, the air was fresh and clean, and the wine was good. One can put up with the encroachments of socialism while these things remain. Under the care of the Admiral's wife and Cecilia, who were determined to equip us suitably for our journey, both *Tzu Hang* and ourselves were soon bursting with good things. We spent 17 days in all in Talcahuano and then sailed for Juan Fernandez. The Admiral and his wife and Cecilia waved to us as we left. We left under sail, close-hauled down the bay and tacking once towards the entrance. For a long time I could see the small figures at the end of the garden watching us go. The Admiral not wanting to sail with us now, yet thinking nostalgically of the days that he had spent at sea and in particular the days in a full-rigged ship on his passages round Cape Horn. He would sail with us in spirit and we would carry his good wishes.

CHAPTER TEN

Juan Fernandez and St Felix

We sailed from Talcahuano for Juan Fernandez on January
20th, in the afternoon, and after passing a large concourse of
pelicans and many other sea-birds in the mouth of the Boca
Chica, worrying at a shoal of fish like a pack of hounds over their
quarry, we were able to set a course directly for the Island, 360
miles away. We did not go far, being becalmed by 2130, with
the land still in sight. By 0300 we had sail up again, with a light
wind from the south. After two quiet days, with light southerly
winds and the genoa set, we sighted Juan Fernandez, two points
off the starboard bow, at a distance of about 40 miles, the tops
of its mountains disappearing into the cloud.

Most of the early adventurers had come here to rest and
recoup their crews, after the passage round Cape Horn, or
through the Straits of Magellan. Alexander Selkirk was
marooned here in 1706 and taken off four years later by the
privateers *Duke* and *Duchess*, which had sailed from Bristol
under Captain Woods Rogers. It was the story of Alexander
Selkirk that led Defoe to write *Robinson Crusoe*, and the Chileans
now call it Robinson Crusoe's Island, hoping to attract
tourists.

The *Centurion* arrived there in 1741. At her first attempt to
find it, her navigators believed that she was too far to the
west, and so stood to the eastwards. It was not until they sighted
the white snows of the Cordillera on the mainland that they
were assured of their mistake and turned westward again. This
delay cost them another 80 of their crew who died from scurvy,
but on the other hand a Spanish fleet of four ships that had been

put in commission was waiting for Lord Anson's fleet, or whatever ships might have survived Cape Horn, with three ships off Concepcion and one off Juan Fernandez. Since no British ships had appeared, they had decided that Lord Anson's fleet was lost and, a day or two before his arrival, they returned to Callao. Anson's crew were in such a desperate condition that it is doubtful whether they would have been able to stand up to even one Spanish warship, so that although the extra delay in reaching the Island cost him 80 men, he might have lost his ship if he had kept on a little longer on his first attempt.

The sloop *Tryal* arrived on the following day in similar condition, the *Gloucester* a month later, so weakly manned that unless Lord Anson had sent out two boats, with fresh provisions and water and a crew to man her, she could never have made port, and finally the pink *Anna* arrived from the shelter that she had found in the Chonos Islands.

As *Tzu Hang* approached the Island, the steep face of the southern slopes, bare and brown, disappeared into the overcast, and a detached islet, Goat Island, also thrust its head into the cloud. It was as well that we had taken care to make our landfall up wind and up current of the Island, for the south wind now freshened and we could see the clouds moving swiftly towards the slopes. Sailing down the north-east coast, with the wind right aft, we dropped all sail but the main, and had to take every care to prevent an involuntary jibe, for the wind, deflected by the cliffs along which we were sailing, hit us first on one quarter and then on the other. The current pushed us along and what with the speed that we were making and the high cliffs that foreshortened the distances, it was hard to judge which point was Punta Baccalau, which marked the southern entrance to Cumberland Bay, until we had actually opened the bay. It was not made any easier by the fact that a small islet off the point, which was marked on the chart, was missing.

As soon as we had identified our bay, helped by two small fishing boats which were heading homeward, we hauled in the main and made for the south-west end of the bay. The clouds poured over the hills, running over the cols and down the valleys, until they detached themselves from the mountain side, spreading and linking at their original level, as they streamed over the bay. The westering sun set them on fire and dazzled our eyes, so that we found it difficult to pick up the landmarks ashore, the pier and the lighthouse, while *Tzu Hang* heeled to violent gusts that came rushing down the valleys. As we came closer and the sun dropped behind the cloud, we were able to see better. We anchored close beside a fleet of small crayfish boats, white double-enders with a high bow and stern and an inboard motor, which looked like a flock of gulls as they lay at their moorings. The anchor went down in seven fathoms, running out 40 fathoms of chain, and in addition we lowered the 20-lb 'Chum' which slides down the chain, to prevent snatching.

The first impression of Juan Fernandez, even from Cumberland Bay, looking at the northern slopes, is that the land will soon be bare, because of the erosion that is taking place. In one or two places there are a few poor gums, which have been planted in an attempt to check it, but the lower slopes of the hills are rapidly being washed away. Up high a short scrub clings to the steep faces, and trees and impenetrable scrub fill the upper valleys, but one might almost say that the land capable of cultivation has already gone. The Chileans are no novices at destroying their land, but it is sad to see destruction still going on. There are some fine trees in and about the village, showing what once grew here, which tend to conceal the shame of the land behind, and it is said that there are still wild figs, apricots and peaches, descendants from the stones that Lord Anson planted.

When Lord Anson arrived it was different.

'However on the 10th, in the afternoon,' writes Walter, the historian of the voyage, 'we got under the lee of the Island, and kept ranging along it at about two miles distance, in order to look out for the proper anchorage, which was described to be in a bay on the north side. And now being nearer in with the shore, we could discover that the broken craggy precipices,

which had appeared so unpromising at a distance, were far
from barren, being in most places covered with woods; and that
between them there were everywhere interspersed the finest
vallies, clothed with a most beautiful verdure, and watered
with numerous streams and cascades, no valley of any extent,
being unprovided of its proper rill. The water too, we afterwards found, was not inferior to any that we had ever tasted
and was constantly clear.'

Walter begins to sound like a modern real estate agent, but
to men dying of scurvy the land, surely as yet unspoiled by
man, must have looked like an earthly paradise. Vegetables
were what they wanted; the first boat ashore on the day of their
arrival brought back quantities of grass which was soon all
eaten. But Walter goes on to describe what they were able to
find when they got ashore.

'Besides a great number of plants of various kinds, which are
to be met with on the Island, but which we were not botanists
enough, either to describe, or to attend to, we found there almost
all the vegetables that are usually esteemed to be particularly
adapted to the cure of those scorbutic disorders, which are
contracted by salt diet and long voyages. For here we had great
quantities of watercresses and purslain, with excellent wild
sorrel, and a vast profusion of turnips and Sicilian radishes. . . .
Besides the vegetables that I have mentioned, of which we made
perpetual use, we found many acres of ground covered with
oats and clover.'

Of all this we saw nothing, but we were not in search of anti-
scorbutics, and particularly not of turnips, but I would have
noticed immediately the oats and clover, seeing only in their
place bare rock and useless sub-soil. Nor did we see anything of
'The woods which covered most of the steepest hills, which were
free from all bushes and underwood, and afforded an easy
passage through every part of them.' Wherever that was so, the
woods have gone.

When Anson, after demolishing the pink *Anna*, left Juan
Fernandez, he caused such havoc up and down the coast, that
the Spanish determined not to again allow any hostile nation

access to the Island. Cumberland Bay was first fortified and a Spanish settlement established in 1749. This was wrecked by an earthquake, which also destroyed Concepcion in Chile, in 1751. The settlement was rebuilt in 1753, but when the Spanish heard of McBride's arrival in the Falkland Islands in 1766, they reinforced it and improved their fortification. When Captain Carteret arrived in 1767, unaware that the Spanish had even occupied the Island, in search of water and fresh vegetables, he found Cumberland Bay buzzing with activity.

'The 8th of May we got a fine gale to ye S.E.,' he wrote in his journal, 'and the 10th made the island of Juan Fernandez, in the afternoon we got close to ye eastern part of it, when we came to haul round ye north end and open Cumberland Bay, I was not a little surprised to observe a great number of men all about the beach, with a house and four pieces of cannon over the waterside with two large boats lying off it, a fort about two or three hundred yards up the rising of a hill on which they hoisted Spanish Colours, it was fased with stones and masonry has eighteen or twenty embrassures with a longhouse inside of it, which I took for barracks for the garrison, it did not seem to be fortified on the back or land side next the hill. All these works were on the westernmost side of the bay; there are round about the fort of different kinds about twentyfive or thirty houses, much cattle feeding on the brow of the hills, which seem to be cultivated, many spots being parted and enclosed. The hard gusts of wind which came right out of the bay hindered our comings so near to it, as I could have desired, for these flows were so violent that we were obliged to let fly our topsail sheets several times for them, alltho close reefed. I think it is not possible for a ship to work in here when the wind blowes hard from the Southward'.

Carteret could see, and reported more, than we could see, but perhaps he himself was up a mast, as when we arrived there were no fields, no visible cultivation, and certainly no cattle feeding on the brows of the hills. But the sea and its problems remain basically the same if you come under sail, as they did 200 years ago. Lord Anson also comments on the winds in Cumberland Bay: 'These frequent and sudden gusts make it difficult for ships to work in with the wind off shore, or to keep a clear hawse when anchored.' From these early descriptions it is interesting to turn to *The South America Pilot Vol. III.* 'Close to the ruined pier,' it says, 'stands a prominent white building, about three hundred yards north westward of which are the ruins of the old fort of San Juan Bautista. . . . From November to May heavy squalls sometimes sweep down the valleys into Cumberland Bay when southerly winds prevail in the vicinity. These squalls have caused vessels to drag their anchors.'

Ours, with the help of the 'Chum', was holding firm, and soon the Port Captain, a vintage lieutenant in the Chilean Navy, came out in one of the crayfish boats that he had temporarily commandeered, and we were free to go ashore. The wind was still whistling off the hills so we decided to leave it until next morning.

Next morning Beryl and I took the dinghy and rowed ashore, leaving Bob happily at work on some small job of maintenance. We pulled the dinghy up on to the rocks of a stony beach half a mile east of the pier and then left the oars at a fisherman's cottage a short way along the narrow footpath, that led back towards the village, close behind the beach. We had a letter of introduction to Señora Blanca, a writer, an artist, and something of a politician, who in self-imposed, or possibily compulsory, exile, had decided to make her home in Juan Fernandez. Our search for her had been delayed by the arrival that morning on *Tzu Hang*, of the loquacious captain of a small motor vessel that plies between Juan Fernandez and Valparaiso, carrying occasional visitors, and bearing the fish and crayfish that are caught on and about the Island back to a market. For visitors there is also a regular air service to a small field, some distance away on the western end of the Island, and passengers are brought from there to Cumberland Bay by boat. At the time that we were there a hotel was in the process of being built, at the head of the eastern arm of the bay, and the few tourists that did arrive stayed in rooms in the village. A visit to Juan

Fernandez is still an adventure, and the Chileans that we were able to recognize as tourists were usually young and happy people, who seemed to be enjoying it.

We found a stream running up a valley, and a footpath following the bank, shaded by tall trees. Anyone whom we met was able to direct us to the house of the Señora for the Señora is a character of some renown. She runs a rambling private hotel, or rather she runs a rambling house and guest cottages to which private, but paying, guests are invited. It is definitely an honour to go there. The rooms wander at different levels, like a creeper that has grown over rocks. They are decorated with all sorts of personal and artistic treasures, and many of Señora Blanca's paintings. There is a Gaugin atmosphere; colour, flowers, sunshine, and shade, and an outside tap and an enamel basin to wash in, which can be emptied into the stream. Above all there is good talk.

When we arrived, at about the hour of siesta, Señora Blanca was sun-bathing, and on being aroused appeared in a Hawaiian hat and wrapped in a large towel which was just tucked together so that, as she showed us round, it looked as if it might descend at any time and leave her stark naked. I was convinced that if this happened she would continue with our tour, with her old-young figure and her old-young blonde hair which showed beneath her strange hat, and that she would ignore the fallen towel and would continue to talk in her youthful and vivacious way without the slightest embarrassment. 'It's you that get embarrassed,' said Beryl, when I told her of my fears. 'You are really most extraordinary about that sort of thing.'

La Señora is the chatelaine of Juan Fernandez and probably the only well-educated person who lives there. She pointed over the picket fence that enclosed her garden, where there are flowers but no grass.

'There is Lord Anson's valley. Here right below my house. That is where he had his tent. He was a very great gentleman,' she said.

I could imagine that she was picturing herself here and Lord Anson there. Like Lord Nelson and Lady Hamilton perhaps.

Lord Anson and La Blanca. But no. She was Chilean. Relations must be humane but cold.

What on earth would Lord Anson think if he saw the valley now. It looked like cement that had been mixed and swirled about, but it was of a reddish-brown colour. There were small hills, eroded waterways, and bare rock and it was contained, as in Lord Anson's time, by two streams, which now carried its soil away. This is Walter's description.

'This piece of ground which he chose was a small lawn, that lay on a little ascent about half a mile from the sea. In front of his tent there was a large avenue cut through the woods to the sea side, which sloping to the water with a gentle descent, opened a prospect of the bay and the ships at anchor. This wood was screened behind by a tall wood of myrtle sweeping round it, in the form of a theatre, the ground on which the wood stood, rising with a much sharper ascent than the lawn itself, though not so much, but that the hills and precipices within land towered up considerably above the tops of the trees, and added to the grandeur of the view. There were besides two streams of chrystal water which ran on the right and left of the tent, within an hundred yards distance, and were shaded by the trees that skirted the lawn on either side, and compleated the symetry of the whole.' It was through some of these trees that we were now looking at the barren desolation that was once a lawn.

Next day we arranged to walk up to Alexander Selkirk's look-out. At least Beryl and Bob were going to walk, but I being no longer able to climb mountains on account of trouble with my knees decided to ride. The pony that carried me was a spindly little thing, which staggered sideways if I lent from the saddle, so that I felt glad that there was no possibility of running into a member of the RSPCA. However, it was game, and climbed like a cat. This time we went on the other side of Anson's valley, and until we got on to the steeper slopes found everywhere the same story of denuded and eroding land. There never has been any control, no wealthy landowners, no government control, and no terracing. If there had been control the land could not look like it does. And it isn't goats that destroy land. It is man, like a cancerous growth on the earth that gives him life; first denuding it of its trees, then of its grass, and then of its soil.

Higher up as the path zigzagged across a spur, or followed the edge of a valley, we began to pass through dense scrub, and here, where it was not too steep for them to grow, there were plenty of trees, particularly in the valleys, but it looks as if only drastic action and lots of money will save the Island.

We found that we were not the only people that were on the way to the look-out, but that we were part of a regular expedition, men, women, and children, most of them on ponies who were on their way to the southern side to kill a steer and bring the beef back to market. From the pass we could see far below us, on the edge of a turquoise sea, where the arid brown earth was in places touched with just a suggestion of green, that cattle were grazing. When Carteret sailed into the bay, he saw 'much cattle feeding on the brow of the hills', but now they could only find grazing on the bare southern slopes.

We were down in time to have lunch with Señora Blanca in her sun-baked garden and to meet Monsieur and Madame Fischer, two famous French photographers, who travel the world photographing 'the eternal verities', whatever they are. They used to photograph more violent things, for they made their name in the Spanish Civil War. They were both most exhilarating people, with important looking cameras dangling all over, one of which was almost perpetually in use. They were embarrassed at the moment by a card that they had had made to send to their hundreds of friends, showing their route which took them to Easter Island, but which they had been unable to reach because the regular tourist flight had been cancelled, and they had come to Juan Fernandez instead. Perhaps it was as well because we heard that Easter Island was just at about the limit of the range of the aircraft that then made it, and a head-wind would put them out of business.

Next day we were ashore again and examined the remains of the Spanish fort that had so surprised Carteret, and found to our delight two old cannon which were being used as bollards on the beach, and were no doubt part of what he had seen. On the top of the fort was a goat, perhaps a descendant of the goat that Anson's crew shot on arrival. Walter, writing about this goat says, 'He [Alexander Selkirk] tells us, amongst other things, as he often caught more goats than he wanted, he sometimes marked their ears and let them go. This was about thirty two years before our arrival on the Island. Now it happened, that the first goat that was killed by our people, at their landing had his ears slit, whence we concluded that he had doubtless been formerly under the power of Selkirk. This was indeed an animal of most venerable aspect, dignified with an exceeding majestic beard, and many other symptoms of antiquity.'

Round the western shore of the bay, and two cables north of where *Tzu Hang* was anchored, was the pier. The water there was invariably too rough to leave the dinghy tied, but a short way away there was a boat ramp, protected by concrete walls, up which the crayfish boats were hauled, when not on their moorings. This ramp was all right for beaching the dinghy in calm weather, and there was never any lack of fishermen or small boys to lend a hand.

At the base of the pier, amongst red fuel drums, we found a saddled mule standing, his reins over his head, his ears pricked, gazing solemnly to sea. On the pier itself a red-cheeked, black-haired girl, dressed in blue jeans and sea boots, was unloading tunny from a fishing boat. The tunny were cut in half for ease of handling so that they showed rounds of firm red meat, like rump steaks, as she placed them in large wicker baskets. Her husband sat on a bench, twiddling a feather lure, and talking to two other fishermen while she worked. The local people, mostly fishermen and their families, looked vigorous and cheerful, were usually good looking, and were as light-skinned as Europeans.

Still farther round the bay we came to a cemetery, as far as it is possible to go, for beyond is Punta San Carlos, the western point. There we found a black stone memorial, with a newly painted life-belt bearing the name of the German cruiser

Dresden placed against the cross, which was surrounded by a rail of anchor chain. It is a memorial to those of her crew who lost their lives, when she was sunk in Cumberland Bay, after escaping from the Battle of the Falkland Islands in the First World War. Her wreck lies in 65 fathoms two cables east of the head of the pier.

We made sail next day, Monday 27th, finding a light westerly wind, and Juan Fernandez disappeared behind cloud at about 30 miles distance, in the evening. In a way we were sorry to leave. In spite of the depressing erosion it seemed to be a happy island, and one well worth visiting.

CHAPTER ELEVEN

To San Felix and the Marquesas

We set *Tzu Hang*'s bow northwards towards San Felix and San Ambrosio, two small and uninhabited islands 420 miles away and 500 miles off the coast. Two hundred years ago Captain Carteret in the *Swallow* was doing the same thing. Like all his predecessors, and like *Tzu Hang* now, he was attracted northwards to the Trade Wind region, 'for there is no such thing as to make a ship go or do anything without a strong fair wind', he wrote in explanation.

The islands of San Felix and San Ambrosio had been discovered first by the same Spaniard who had found and named Juan Fernandez, and had been sighted later by Davis on his privateering voyage, but he had reported them as being 500 leagues, rather than miles, off the South American coast. The cartographers of that time, who were endeavouring to piece together a chart of the Pacific on little information, had linked these islands with Rogeveen's Easter Island, and had begun to etch in a southern continent in this area, which they called Davis Land. Carteret's search for Davis Land was unsuccessful, and since he found nothing but sea where it was supposed to be, the myth of a southern continent in this locality wilted and died.

We knew that the islands were uninhabited, that a number of brown and blue-faced boobies nested on them, and that fishermen had sometimes used them as a temporary base, particularly San Felix, where we heard that two cats had been left. These cats, on a diet of rats, eggs, and young boobies, were said to have grown very large, and we hoped to see them. We also knew that the only landing place was on the north-western end of San Felix, and that it could only be used in fine weather.

Even if we found on arrival that we could not get ashore, this route was taking us into the Trade Winds and into the west-going current. If we had chosen to visit Easter Island and Pitcairn, both on the direct route to the Marquesas, we would have had to put up with lighter winds and neither of them have very safe anchorages. Our object had been to round Cape Horn on a return voyage to Canada and now none of us wanted to be deflected into more leisurely or extended cruising. We wanted to get home with least delay.

We had light winds all that first day, and a quiet night, and brought down all sail at about two in the morning. At eight o'clock, with Juan Fernandez still in sight, the motor was started. Apart from the fact that we motored all day, it was a lovely day, with the horizon all round so well defined that I felt as if I could see the curvature of the earth's surface wherever I looked. During the morning a large whale passed us some distance away and steaming north-west. We saw noticeably fewer now than we did when we first started cruising. A breeze came from the west in the evening and went round to the south. We set the port staysail and the main to starboard, and *Tzu Hang* steered herself throughout a faultless night; moon-light, a gentle wind, and a wealth of stars.

On the following morning the wind began to freshen. We jibed the main and set the staysail to starboard, altering course slightly to keep the sails filled. Next day *Tzu Hang* was running in fine style with storm petrels playing round the log line and treading the water with one dangling foot, like someone testing the temperature of a bath. We sighted the Islands by 1200 and were up to San Felix by 1630. It is a strange island, a mixture of yellow cliffs and black lava, and about a mile and a half long with its western end 630 feet high.

Several miles off we were greeted by the boobies. One of them kept diving on the log spinner but always misjudged the speed and hit the water a little aft. He looked very indignant and went off to have a few practise runs on fish, then returned again to the spinner, but with the same unsatisfactory results. Another, gliding too close under the lee of the mainsail, was deprived of his wind and pitched into the sea. He looked so ridiculously put out at the shabby trick that he thought we had played him, that we all three burst out laughing.

Round behind the western end of the island we discovered the landing place, by a black lava cave, just where the lava joins the yellow cliff. A rope hand-rail was fixed there, which had been used by the fishermen to climb the cliff. Unfortunately, the fresh Trade Wind that we had had all day was sending a swell round both sides of the island and I could find no bottom with the lead as we came in. I knew that I should find it a little farther in shore, and if I had been in Norway or British Columbia, I should not have hesitated to have gone right in, dropped the anchor close to the cliffs and got a line from the stern to the shore, but there was something about this ocean swell sucking against the rocks, and the islands being so far out at sea and so deserted, that I found that I did not like to bring *Tzu Hang* so close in. After two attempts I gave it up and Beryl at any rate, who doesn't like rocks, was happy.

Now we were fairly embarked on our Pacific crossing. We had 3,400 miles to go, about 1,100 miles longer than the normal Atlantic crossing from the Canaries, and our course would take us between Easter Island and the Galapagos Islands, 2,000 miles apart. It was February 1st, and for the first two days we had an easy wind. No wonder that this huge expanse of water is called the Pacific. Watch followed watch and day followed day with hardly a change of sail; in fact between February 11th and 26th we did not touch a sail at all. At night *Tzu Hang* seemed to dance along, and all around her there seemed to be a rustling and a patter of dancing feet.

In latitude 16°S and about 1,200 miles from San Felix we first began to notice that the current was helping us, and from then on we had a lift of about 13 miles a day. The current was by no means regular and on two successive days we had a contrary current of eight miles on each day. We were averaging about five knots by day and a little less at night. The log shows

the uneventful passage, when almost every entry has something
to do with the cat or the sea birds that we saw.

Date	Time	Log	Remarks	
Feb 13	0400	1445	Pwe has been up all night. One flying fish.	
	1820	1520	Today's escort of tropic birds. Two young ones— black bills. Saw a whale this evening. Now sailing herself. Wind very light.	Lat at noon 15°20'S
Feb 14	0000	1552	Overcast. Sailing herself.	
	0430	1573		
	1215	1609		Lat at noon 14°48'S

(Sometimes I put the noon position and the distance run by
observation in the log but usually it is only marked on the
chart.)

	1640	1625	Pwe very sick after eating too many flying fish. Thought she had enteritis.

By day the sun shone through serried ranks of Trade Wind
clouds, by night the moon waxed and waned, and the southern
stars that we had become accustomed to wheeled across the
sky. For the whole of the passage there was never a high flying
jet to be heard, nor a ship to be seen. Nor was there a threat of
bad weather, nor doubt of position to disturb us. The endless
sea rolled on, and *Tzu Hang* with it, reeling off her 120 miles a
day, as the little black spots on the back of an old chart, on
which I had marked off this portion of the Pacific, crept towards
their goal. We could not even be worried about discovering
Taihoe Bay in Nuku Hiva, because Bob had been there before.

By day we saw sometimes a congregation of sea-birds diving
and calling over a shoal of fish, by night, as the stars climbed
over us, we heard sometimes the call of a tropic bird, sometimes

the harsher cry of a tern, the splash of a fish breaking the surface of the water, or the breathing of porpoises about the boat, as they drew their phosphorescent lines across our bow.

It was hot in the afternoon, from lunch until three, when it was hard to find shade. Then Bob or I, on watch, would sluice down the deck and ourselves at the same time. Apart from these two hours the heat was never uncomfortable. We read enormously and ate well. Two eggs, bacon, toast, butter, home-made marmalade and coffee or Chinese tea for breakfast; an orange at about ten, or orange juice, or coffee; lunch of home-made bread, various cheeses, and fresh salad—onions, tomatoes, and cabbage—salami and sardines. Dinner of two courses, always cooked by Bob, both of which, except for the potatoes, came out of a tin. A glass of wine for lunch and dinner, and a cocktail at 1800, two on Sundays, or to celebrate each thousand miles.

On February 28th we were getting towards the end of our long passage, but were plagued by light Trades. We flopped about all night, rolling what little wind there was out of the sails, although on Bob's watch, because he is a patient helmsman, they were quiet. On Beryl's watch some leviathan came rushing up behind *Tzu Hang* so close that she thought it was going to hit us, but she was unable to see what it was. There were signs of increasing marine and bird life, with many terns crying about the ship. At noon on March 1st we found that the log spinner had gone, taken by some fish. For a time we had a big marlin accompanying us, and at other times during the day numbers of small tunny, and in the evening, 200 miles away from land, we saw a frigate bird. These birds are supposed always to spend the night ashore. This one had a long way to go, it was already late, and he did not appear to be heading homewards.

On Sunday, March 2nd, we saw two more frigate birds and our noon position showed that we were 70 miles from Ua Huka Island. I announced that we would sight it that night at 0100, but whilst having our drink in the cockpit that evening Bob saw the Island against the sunset clouds, fine on the starboard bow. We passed it, sailing about four miles off its south coast at 0300 next morning, so that, if Bob had paid more attention to his drink and less to the horizon, I might have been just right. It stood dark and silent beside us as we passed, with no lights showing, and when day broke the hills of Nuku Hiva were already large in front of us, and soon took on details of form and colour.

Nuku Hiva is only 30 miles from Ua Huka so that we were arriving in good time. It stretched in front of us, a panorama of steep and strangely shaped cliffs, of green and grey peaks rising to a height of 3,000 feet, and a high plateau in the centre. The harbour of Taihoe Vae is right in the middle of the southern side of the Island, and turns to the north-east as it is entered, so that it is well protected from the south-east Trade Winds. The entrance, which is not entirely visible as a ship approaches from the south-east, being marked by a rocky spur on one side and a detached islet of grey rock on the other. Bob had no difficulty in recognizing it. The only danger on this side is the rock, Teohote Kea, off the south-eastern point of the island, Cape Tikapo, which might be hard to pick up at night, but which our course had given a wide berth.

As we rounded the point and came in to the harbour we lost the wind, but were able to continue under sail to the anchorage, where a Tahitian ketch was lying; she had come in a few days before from Los Angeles after a 21-day passage, having carried a good wind all the way. A beach ran round the head of the bay, backed by coconut trees, and behind this a road, close under the hills which rose steeply behind it. Towards the eastern end of the head of the bay there was a long pier and at its head a small, white motor vessel was moored, an inter-island passenger and freight ship, whose Marquesan captain later gave me an old chart of the Islands. Behind the pier the road rose to higher ground where some substantial buildings could be seen, amongst casuarinas, hibiscus, and bougainvillaea. This was the end where the upper ranks of the Island hierarchy were established, the government offices and the post office and the police station. At the western end of the bay the road disappeared into a darker and more lowly greenness, past humbler homes.

Along the road and on the pier were one or two bright dresses, and I, fresh from reading Typee, imagined them clinging in the soft wind to the slender brown-skinned figures of lovely Fayaways, bare-footed and strong-toed, with long dark hair cascading down their shoulders, a flower behind their ears. They were not there when we got ashore, and most of the island beauties must be in Tahiti. Instead we found broad-hipped and heavy matrons, wearing European cotton dresses and straw hats, who rode small motorcycles or mopeds to the village store, little buzzing things, half-hidden between the thighs of the rider.

The stores in the village were dark and stuffy, smelling of stale wine. Rows of print dresses behind a tin-topped counter hung between shelves of men's shirts, of bathing shorts from Japan, and white cotton vests. The floor was cluttered with sacks of sweet potatoes, boxes of cabbages, and cases of canned beer; the walls with fishing tackle, cane knives, and other tools. Outside the women who had finished their shopping were sitting on the grass at a road corner playing Bingo.

The mopeds, the print dresses, and the shoddy tin-roofed European-type houses may be a sign of an improved standard of living but there are few people now to fill the valleys of the Happars and Typees. I had an impression of dissolution and degradation which the sunshine and the shade, the blue of the sea, the scarlet and yellow flowers, the green trees, and even the mountains themselves and the white clouds coursing above them could not dispel.

Beryl and I went to the Gendarmerie to get our clearance, and were asked if we had a lifeboat on board, as required by regulations. Fortunately we had the Avon dinghy, stowed in the stern behind Bob's bunk, and impossible to get at in a hurry.

'And life-belts for all on board?'

It was Beryl who remembered the small plastic models from Montevideo.

The two policemen, one from Tahiti, and one from France, who were taking over and handing over the station, glanced at each other, both large and good looking men.

'*Alors*,' said one.

'*Bon voyage*,' said the other. 'You have permission to visit Typee Vae and you may leave from there when you wish, but before ten days.'

It was all very simple, and a new procedure, as till recently visiting yachts have had to enter and clear in Tahiti. We went back to *Tzu Hang* and spent some time in the sea, scrubbing at her bottom to remove the goose-necked barnacles that covered it, each of us with an attendant file of little fishes, who jostled for scraps as they floated away. Bob then went for one of his strenuous, barefoot walks halfway up the hills towards the plateau. I picked him up in the evening at the pier where women and children had been fishing and catching small fish about three inches long for their evening meal. The most industrious and successful were half-Japanese.

We were sitting just before dark in the cockpit. The lightest of breezes sought us with a sweet smell of flowers from the shore. The bay was deserted now except for *Tzu Hang*, and only a few lights showed from the houses on the hill, for the lower village did not have electricity. The first stars were showing, the heat had gone from the day, and the mountains stood steep and dark above us, and incredibly still. From the shore came the voice of a girl singing. The Islands have their moments and this was one of them.

We left next morning for Typee Vae, with a gusty wind to help us out from the anchorage, and we were soon able to go on the starboard tack and to sail up the coast, close off shore. The entrance to Typee Vae is immediately west of the south-eastern cape, Cape Tikapo. As we approached it we could see the sea breaking on the half-submerged rock, Te Ohote Kea, so that it looked like a black motor boat coming fast towards us. Cape Tikapo is a narrow peninsula, with a vertical wall of rock on its eastern side, perpetually battered by the Trade Wind seas. Its ridge is about 1,000 feet high, with a frieze of strangely shaped rocks, like prehistoric animals, along its crest, and the point encloses a wide, three-fingered bay, the centre finger being the longest and leading to Typee Vae. Well up towards the head of the sound there is a small warehouse and a stone quay, and it was off this quay that we anchored. From there it was possible to row up the river, after crossing a shallow bar, or to take the footpath from the wharf, which runs along the side of the hill and later follows the valley to the village of Typee, a mile away.

Bob, when he was here before, had walked over from Taihoe Vae, and had met Madame Clarke, a Marquesan, whose Tahitian husband had left her and returned to Tahiti. Bob took Beryl up to the village to meet her and to arrange for a horse for me so that we could go next day on an expedition to see the old Tikis and Holy Places on the hill above the village. Madame Clarke arrived next morning riding a pony. She had a narrow, tragic face, with a look about it of an American Indian, and she had slightly bowed legs, and walked like a hillman, but with her toes turned in. She wore purple stretch trousers and a green jersey, and her hair was tightly coiled and tied with red ribbon. She was middle aged, smoked incessantly, and had a desperate hacking cough, so that she sounded as if she had the disease, which, amongst others, had thinned the valley. She had a grand manner, that of a 'grande seigneure'.

Beryl and she went in front and I rode behind, feeling embarrassed at being on pony-back while they walked. There was no need. Round the next bend I met a Marquesan gentleman, riding, while his women walked ahead. We followed the path above the sea arm and then along the stream. The waves were breaking over a wide shingle bar at its mouth and I could see that it would need some judgement to get the dinghy through. Beyond the bar the river wandered through a valley, splitting and joining again round sand banks and islands. The land looked fabulously rich, for the good soil has been taken off the mountains and desposited on its floor. Later we met a Frenchman who had retired there and become a market gardener.

'You can grow anything,' he said. 'Look at my garden. It is just that these Marquesans are so hopeless. They are so idle. Only coconuts and pigs. Faugh!'

'Then you must have a problem in getting all this lovely produce to a market?' asked Beryl.

'Yes', he admitted, 'that is a problem indeed. But a market will come no doubt.'

Meanwhile Madame Clarke led us through a wide valley of coconut trees, past gardens where avocados and papayas grew wild and where pigs rootled. Until the population increases there seems no need for them to forsake their natural foods and toil for cabbages, onions, and chard.

'Do you own much of this land?' I asked Madame Clarke.

Apparently she did. 'Typee Vae—c'est moi,' she said in de Gaullic style.

We found the Tikis and the old Maraes deserted and buried beneath scrub and coarse grass on the tops of the hills and in one shack in the valley, where we took shelter because of a douwnpour of rain, a door was propped open with the head of a broken Tiki.

When we got back to the boat Madame Clarke looked exhausted. After a glass or two of whisky, some of which she poured on to tissue paper and applied as a poultice to her breast, which she said was paining her, she became determined to show Bob and Beryl a cave on the cliffs of Cape Tikapo, which had been a holy place. They set off in the dinghy and I watched the steady stroke of the oars until the dinghy was dwarfed to nothing by the height of the cliffs, and only the splash of an oar showed sometimes, as if a gull had dived. It was dark by the time they were back, and Madame Clarke took her pony and rode off up the trail to her lonely cough ridden night. She had been unable to recognize the cave from the sea, and Bob and Beryl went off to seek it by land next morning, but without result. Next day, March 9th, we set sail for Hilo.

As we left Typee Vae, the Trade Wind was gusting directly into it, in a manner that made us suppose that it might be blowing freshly outside. *Tzu Hang* tacked round Teaohote Kea, the black rock at the entrance on which the waves were breaking, and came back to within half a mile of the huge cliffs of Cape Tikapo, that rise so steeply from the sea. We were on the weather side, so close to the cliffs that the up-draught affected our wind, as if it was dragging the whole blanket of the Trade Winds over our heads leaving us wallowing in the swell that rebounded off the steep rock wall.

We started the motor and crept along under the cliffs. Beryl and Bob looked their disapproval, and if the motor had stopped we would have been in an unpleasant situation, for the rough sea emptied our sails of any wind that might reach them. Their disapproval was so obvious that I refused to notice it, and the motor ran well in my support, so that we were soon past the rock wall and found the wind blowing at sea level again following the lead of another valley which opened up as we passed down the coast. The freshening wind and the swift current sent us quickly on our way.

Our course was north to the equator along the 140th meridian in order to get a good slant for Hawaii when we met the northeast Trade Winds, and we steered a little east of north in order to counteract the set of the current. By 1800 we could see the dim outlines of both Eiao and Hatutu, the northerly islands of the Marquesas, and I wondered at times during the night, as I listened for the sound of breakers or the call of sea-birds, whether I had given the Isle du Sable a wide enough berth. We neither saw nor heard anything of it. There were many porpoises around us and we could hear them from below again giving their high-pitched whistles. I have often tried to attract them by blowing a whistle on the deck, with absolutely no result, but perhaps those silent dog whistles would be more effective.

The day broke with the wind in the north-east, as it had been the day before. Before sunrise three boobies came flying out of the west from the direction of the Isle du Sable, low and purposefully intent on reaching some private fishing ground of their own. I could see their ill-tempered faces, for boobies never look happy, as they slipped along the crests of the wave, their white wings with black tips just clearing the dull water.

On Wednesday, March 12th, the sun was right overhead at noon so that the angle remained the same in whichever direction the sextant was pointed. The horizon was clear all round and *Tzu Hang* seemed to be suspended from the very centre of the dome of the sky. The north-east wind that had come in while we were still off Nuku Hiva freshened so that we made good time, but next day it was more in the east and the starboard staysail was boomed out. The equator was crossed at longitude 141° 40′. Every morning a satellite winged its way across the sky with the regularity of a businessman on his way to the station, except that it was exactly 20 minutes later each day. On March 15th we were into unsettled weather although the wind stayed in the east, and the next day we hit the Inter-Tropical Convergence Zone, or in other words, the Doldrums, but Doldrums with plenty of wind.

In the early morning, as daylight came, it showed massive clouds piled in front of us, where the lightning had been flickering all night. There was no chance to discover the business-man satellite today. Our latitude was 5°N. The rain was soon cascading down and it rained all day as if the tanks above us would never run dry, and it rained all night, too. In oilskins with the hoods up and towels tied round our necks the water still found its way inside, and to steady oneself with a hand to the shrouds was to invite a stream of water up an oilskin sleeve. The wind dropped with the sun so that *Tzu Hang* motored, sopping, through the night. With daylight came a violent rain squall which left us with a split in the leach, so that we decided the Japanese sail had had its day, and set the Cape Horn mainsail again. With the wind fresh from the north-east *Tzu Hang* sailed herself, and we set our course for a point 100 miles east of Hawaii in order to give plenty of allowance for the Trade Wind drift.

On Wednesday 19th we were still sailing fast, the helmsman continually soaked with rain and spray, and everything damp below, not from any specific leak, but from wet oilskins, wet feet and condensation. A strong Trade Wind was blowing so that during the night we had reefed both mizzen and main. These were conditions on which *Tzu Hang* thrived and she had been doing over 160 miles a day, with the log humming, but at

15°N we ran out of grey skies and into sunshine and, at the same time, the wind eased.

We still had hopes of making Hilo on Sunday the 23rd but the wind continued light and although we had the genoa up we could barely make 100 miles a day. On Sunday morning, just as the first tinge of colour appeared in the sky, I saw the lights of a ship crossing astern. It was the first sign that we were approaching land, and the first ship that we had seen since a Japanese ore-carrier had passed us near San Felix, the first in 6,000 miles. Daylight came to show us cloud ahead which we supposed concealed Hawaii, although we were still 60 miles away, and in the afternoon we could make out its massive shape. Soon after dark we saw the light at Cape Kumahi and since we had not far to go we let *Tzu Hang* jog on during the night crossing one of her old trails, with only her mainsail set. We had averaged 130 miles a day from Nuku Hiva and were now content to take our time.

In the morning we were off Hilo. We motored in between two dark rain squalls that passed each side of us and trailed over the cultivated hills behind the port.

'What is that green stuff?' I said.

'Sugar,' said Beryl. 'It looks like the hills north of Durban, doesn't it?'

'Of course it is. And there's the mill. Do you remember? Right behind the Coastguard basin?'

'Is that the basin?' asked Beryl.

'Yes,' said Bob. 'Behind that ship at the wharf.'

Buildings, hotels, shopping centres, and houses had transformed the edges of the big bay, but the entrance to the Coastguard basin was the same. We tied up with our stern to the wall as we had done on our first visit and soon John and Mary Lavery, who had also circumnavigated the world eastabout in their yacht *Sitisi*, were on board with a huge mail. *Sitisi* was sold, and John was now busy changing the appearance of Hilo, building several houses at once, with a view to building another yacht and setting off round the world again.

It rained every day in Hilo and as there was no chance of

doing any painting or of dolling up *Tzu Hang* for her return to Canada, we took her round the coast through the Alenuihaha Channel on the south-west side of Hawaii, to an almost deserted port called Kawaihai. Here is a sugar factory, a small boat harbour, a fine breakwater, and tucked in to the south-eastern corner, behind the breakwater, four dolphins and a short pier, army property, with a notice calling attention to its privacy, which John Lavery had told us to ignore.

We had a fine sail round to the south coast, leaving in the evening, and by the time it was dark the whole land was hidden by rain. Soon the night was so black that I began to regret that we had not streamed the log. We were well equipped with charts again, lent to us by various friendly yachtsmen in Hilo, but we had to estimate the distance run before turning down the channel. There was not a sign of light or land but only dark rain squalls to leeward until *Tzu Hang* was into the channel, when the weather cleared and with it all kinds of lights shone out suddenly, marking the north-western point of Hawaii. With the wind dead aft we raced down the channel with only the main set. *Tzu Hang* seemed to be exulting in the renewal of her liberty like a dog let off the leash. She was trying to tell us that she had had quite enough rest for the time being.

We rounded the point in fine style and, keeping about a mile off shore, headed along the coast for Kawaihai. Although it was still raining and blowing on the north side, here on the south side it was clear, with stars and lights showing, but the wind volleyed down the gullies from the mountains, heeling *Tzu Hang* and sending her spinning along through the calm water. We were in soon after daylight, when the wind had dropped but since now we knew how hard it could blow off the mountains, we laid an anchor towards them, across the channel, dropping it close to the reef, and then pulled *Tzu Hang* back and secured her stern to a dolphin half a cable from the army pier.

All over the world people tend to believe that it can blow harder in home waters, or that the seas may be worse or the currents stronger, than anywhere else in the world. The yachtsmen of Hawaii are no exception. Those who live in Hawaii itself are apt to believe that the Alenuihaha channel is the worst in the Islands, and those who live in Oahu affirm that the strongest winds are found in the Molokai channel. Probably the Alenuihaha is the worst, because of the high mountains on each side of it, but the Molokai is the best known, because of the 'Trans Pac' race, which is approaching its finish here, as the yachts race for Diamond Head, and since no one would dream of shortening sail so near the finish, away go the spinnakers and sometimes the masts as well. It is quite possible that they get the strongest winds of the whole race in this channel.

For those who have come from higher latitudes, the passages between the Islands are short, and though the wind may be fresh and boisterous, it doesn't appear to have the weight of colder air.

'Where are you from?' Any visitor to the Ala Wei Yacht Harbour is bound to be asked the question, and the answer may be, 'From Vancouver', or 'Melbourne', or possibly 'Cape Horn', an intolerably arrogant reply.

'Had a good trip,' will be the next question.

'Yes. Very good.'

'What did you think of the Molokai Channel?'

The right answer to this is 'Pretty tough', or at least something like it.

We spent nearly three weeks in Kawaihai harbour, left almost alone except for occasional visits from our friend in Hilo. On the north-east coast the rain clouds came piling up, bringing small boat warnings, but on our side they had invariably spilled their rain before they reached us and the remnants drifted over, spent and empty, and quite unable to hide the sun. Looking from seawards towards the saddle between the great volcanoes, from which our weather came, there was a regular line where only a mile or two from the shore, the brown stony land, covered with thorny scrub and bright with sunshine, turned to green pasture and ranch-land shadowed by the cloud, and often under rain. Amongst the thorns along the seashore were chukor and black partridge and I loved to hear their call in the early morning. Both had been imported, and the chukor were doing well, the black not so well established.

It was a most profitable time, during which we rested and painted and bathed and *Tzu Hang* began to shine under Bob's patient work. He hid the naked glass fibre on the mainmast with two coats of white, painted the hull again from the dinghy, and even made a good effort at the white waterline. Considering her topsides had only been painted in the water since we had left America two years before she was soon looking remarkably spruce. The days were not always painting days and usually in the afternoon the wind was too strong and the bay too sloppy to do much from the dinghy. Then Bob turned his attention to getting the last of Captain Varela's glass fibre off the deck, or we scraped the hull under water in an attempt to get off the goose barnacles that had survived our scrubbings in Nuku Hiva, although they didn't appear to have interfered much with her speed.

At the end of two weeks even Bob began to think that she was about ready for another appearance in public and even for her return to Canada.

We sailed one night for Lahaina with Penny Brown and Dick Solmensen on board for the trip. We had moved out during the afternoon from our dolphins and lay at anchor in the harbour while we went up to dinner at Kamuela. When we arrived back we were glad to find *Tzu Hang* still in the same place. It had been blowing hard all afternoon, but ashore the rain and the movement of the trees and the small boat warning on the north coast had made us feel guilty for leaving her at anchor in a new place, with no one on board. There she was as usual, patiently waiting for us, the white masts reflecting the shore lights. We soon had the dinghy on board, the main up, the mizzen backed, the jib ready for hoisting. The anchor came up cleanly and *Tzu Hang* began to move off slowly on the right tack as we hauled and set the jib, and soon we were slipping along quietly towards the buoys that marked the harbour entrance.

Dick Solmenson was headmaster of a boys' school and he seemed to be just the man for the job as he loved all that the land had to offer there. Surf-riding, mountaineering, ski-ing, shooting, riding and sailing. As he told us with enthusiasm of all that he did it sounded as if he was running an 'Outward Bound' course rather than a regular boys' school. Penny Brown, with an athletic figure and a boyish enthusiastic face, married and with a young family, wanted some experience in a bigger yacht before she and her husband bought one and took the family sailing. At first the cockpit seemed crowded with Dick and Penny determined to see as much as they could, and as we got into the Alenuihaha Channel equally determined to keep on deck for other reasons. Neither of them succumbed to seasickness and later in the night Dick was able to go below, wedging himself in a seat immediately below the sliding hatch.

During my watch, with *Tzu Hang* sailing fast and a beam sea, Penny was sitting on the lee side of the cockpit. I enjoyed my new audience and the watch passed very quickly as I told her tall tales of the sea. Penny lent towards me as the boat heeled. At this moment on many occasions a wet wave top splashed over my shoulders and, with concentrated venom, straight for the open neck of Penny's oilskins. She was too wet and cold to bother much about it, but she must have shipped gallons during my watch alone. It was a rough introduction to sailing in a bigger boat, but she was so obviously made of the right stuff for a sailor, that I have no doubt that her husband has by now bought a bigger yacht.

Nights like this for all of us come to an end, and the end of this one must have been especially welcome to Penny and Dick. By daylight we were already in calmer water and soon the sun came out, and breakfast, and warmth, and the sight of beaches and green hills. It was still gusty weather with white horses all over the place. After looking at the entrance to a shallow yacht harbour, on the south side of Maui's low neck, we decided it was altogether too windy to attempt it, so continued along the coast till we were a few miles from Lahaina. There we anchored for lunch, still not quite out of the wind, and then

found that only a mile or so farther the wind had gone altogether. These are the Lahaina roads, once so much used by
whalers, but we put in to the narrow little yacht harbour and
tied up stern to the breakwater. It was absolutely still.

Next morning, ashore to see Penny and Dick off, I was standing beside an old whaling boiler once used for boiling blubber,
when I felt myself being nudged by a sunshade handle and
turned round to find myself confronted by a very over-
decorated tourist. 'Will you tell me what this pot is?' she asked.

'A giant's pot,' I replied, as this seemed to be the quickest
way of disposing of her.

'Now don't tell me,' she said coyly. 'I know who you are.
You're that famous English actor.'

Which one could that be? Perhaps it is just as well that I shall
never know.

When we came to leave Lahaina we went a little too far
across the channel in order to clear the yacht beside us and
stuck on the mud. At this moment the catamaran designer and
expert sailor, Carter Pyle, arrived with a small outboard so
that we were able to throw him a line which he took ashore to a
bollard and we winched off. It was all done so promptly that I
don't think anyone who saw it thought it other than a well
planned manœuvre to get a largish yacht out of a small anchorage. That's what I hope anyway.

From Lahaina *Tzu Hang* went round to Honolua Bay on the
north-west coast. It is very sheltered here, provided that you
go far enough in. When the wind is blowing strongly breakers
come rolling in on each side of the bay, and from outside it
looks a poor anchorage. As we entered we could see that the
breakers did not stretch right across the harbour and well
inside the water was calm except for a gentle swell. Only on
very rare occasions will the seas break right across and then it
is no place to stay in. The road climbs up the cliffs on each side
of the bay, so that we could get lovely views of *Tzu Hang* from
all angles as she lay still below us. There were no houses there
but a good beach for landing on at the head of the bay backed
by palm trees, and behind this a stream of fresh water.

It is a great place for surfing, not actually in the bay, but off one of the points that enclose it. From the cliffs above we got a splendid view of the surfers as they came rushing in, apparently straight for the cliffs on which we were standing. With their brightly coloured swimming shorts and boards, as they lay a couple of hundred yards or more off the point, waiting for the right wave, they reminded me of jockeys waiting at the start before they have come under starter's orders.

The swell came rolling in and one after another the boards lifted and dipped disdainfully as they passed. Then suddenly there was activity as several of the surfers selected a wave together, and turned their boards towards the shore. The wave picked them up and shot them forward leaving one or two who had misjudged their timing behind at the start. Almost at once two or three were up and standing on their boards, their feet moving quickly as they adjusted their balance. Then they came flying in. One lost his balance and pitched into the water and his board flew high into the air and landed near him as his head reappeared, another lost his balance and his board which came racing in on the front of the wave straight for the rocks below. Then only one was left, in the tunnel, that is just under the curl of the breaking crest. He paddled with his hand along the face of the wave on the front of which he was riding in an endeavour to keep just out of the breaking water, then he stood erect again, flying over rocks that appeared almost bare beneath his board until he suddenly let the wave ride on without him and sank into the water behind.

It is a very exciting sport to watch and so must be a particularly thrilling one to take part in. No wonder it gets hold of young people so that they can think of nothing else and only live to follow the surf wherever it may be reported as rolling in and suitable for their play.

One day in *Tzu Hang* I heard girlish laughter and splashing near the ship and a girl's voice complaining that there was a fish in her bikini. I went on deck and found two girls swimming in home-made bikinis, one of whom was in distress about the fish.

'It must be a very small fish,' I said, 'you'd better come on board and shake it out.'

When they came on board, looking brown, fit, and attractive, I found that one was the daughter of an officer in the army and one of a business man, but that they had turned from the orthodox life and come to Hawaii. Here, like camp followers of old, they followed the army of bobbed and golden-haired young surfers, so bronzed and athletic, who spend their days in the sea. They sold them lemon squash and home-made cakes and bread on the beaches.

'You can sell anything here, provided it's good,' one girl told Beryl.

'Well, you can sell me some of your home-made bread.'

They came next day, just before we left, with six loaves, for which Beryl gave them six dollars. 'What were you going to charge me?' she asked them after they had accepted.

'Well,' they said, 'we had talked about it, and we thought a dollar a loaf, but then we had decided that we wouldn't charge you anything.'

From Honolua Bay we had a fast sail across the channel to Molokai, along the north coast of Molokai looking for an anchorage but the Trade Wind was blowing so freshly that we thought it best to leave it alone and so continued across the Molokai channel and into the yacht harbour at Alawai just as night fell.

A month later, just after getting our clearance for Victoria from the Harbourmaster I came back to *Tzu Hang*, to find Bob with a long face.

'There's something very wrong with B,' he said. 'She's been sick and seems to be in great pain.'

I hurried below in fear and anxiety, for she never admits to sickness, and found her coiled up in agony on her bunk.

CHAPTER TWELVE

The Road Home

We have always taken our health so much for granted on *Tzu Hang*, that we have rarely thought of serious illness striking while at sea, or of the need for urgent surgical care. Both of us feel that since we sail for pleasure, we haven't the right to call for assistance when it may involve others, possibly in danger and certainly in inconvenience, should they come to our aid.

We do not carry a radio transmitter for this reason, partly because of the extra equipment and expense involved and partly because we do not like them. I have sometimes been asked if I consider it more sporting to travel such long distances without one, but of course I don't. It is only this mild matter of principle that we should not involve others in our misfortunes, but rather face them by ourselves. Only once before has *Tzu Hang* had serious illness on board, when a friend who was sailing with us went down suddenly in the night with a perforated ulcer. There had been no previous warning and it was perhaps due to taking too many pain-stoppers too quickly to ease a violent toothache, but luckily *Tzu Hang* had arrived in a port where there were hospitals and doctors available. In case it should be suggested that we were glad enough to get help then—indeed we were, but we did not ask the hospital to come to *Tzu Hang*.

Beryl above all people, who will never admit to illness while she can stand on her own feet, who would never accept that she has a right to call for assistance while at sea, would be the last person to ask for help. Now she was in dire need of it, and *Tzu Hang*, our lucky *Tzu Hang*, was again in port.

A few days before this I had met an English doctor, Jack

Watson, who was working in Honolulu. He owned a 'Cal 28' and Bob had been racing with him during our stay. 'If ever you are in need of medical assistance,' he said to me, 'let me know, and I should be so glad to help.'

'Thank you so much,' I replied, 'but we seem to be pretty healthy. I certainly will if we need it.'

Now we did and I telephoned to him at the hospital.

'Well,' he said, 'I am sorry to hear that, but I am not the man for you. I only go down to the throat. Bring her along as soon as you can to the emergency entrance here and I will have a good surgeon, Bob Peyton, also a sailing man, to meet her there. He's a specialist in this sort of thing and you could not find a better. He will look after her. I will be there to meet you too.'

I went back to Beryl and told her what I'd arranged, and said that I'd ring up for an ambulance. She rallied enough, although she was still in very severe pain, to tell me what she thought of that idea. Ambulances were out, but I had seen enough badly wounded soldiers to know that she was very ill indeed. I started ashore to borrow one of the cars that had been offered for our use, but as I stepped hurriedly on deck, I was met by a friend, who said brightly: 'I've just come to take Beryl to buy her fresh stores before you leave.'

'Thank God,' I said. 'You can take her to the hospital instead.'

In a very short time we had pulled *Tzu Hang* alongside the jetty and handed poor Beryl, all doubled up with pain, down over the side and into a car.

At the hospital all went swiftly. Bob Peyton, tall and good-looking, a 'Doctor Kildare' if ever there was one, soon had Beryl in his hands. After examining her he called me in.

'I can't tell you exactly what it is,' he said, 'until I've had a look inside. But I can tell you this. She has an a-cute stomach. And when I say an a-cute stomach I mean an a-cute stomach, and not a cute stomach.' He touched Beryl gently. 'It may be her gall bladder, it may be a perforated appendix, but we've got to operate immediately. She's as hard as a board here.'

I saw to my relief that Beryl, who usually professes to be against operations in general, was as putty in his hands. She was in no shape to offer resistance. On our way from Nuku Hiva she had developed a boil on her arm which had opened up into a large sore. She kept it bandaged up but it had not healed and any other scratch tended to go sceptic. Bob and I had lived with it so long that I forgot it when talking to Jack Watson, but now the bandage was off and Bob Peyton turned his attention to it.

'What worries me,' he said, 'is how the devil we're ever going to get her disinfected. Look at her. She's simply dripping in puss.'

A nurse arrived with swabs, forceps and disinfectant. 'You'll have to leave her now,' Bob said. 'Come back at two and I'll be able to tell you how things have gone.'

I kissed her sweaty forehead and left her to his care.

At two o'clock, after an age of anxiety, I was pacing fretfully up and down the hospital waiting-room, when Bob Peyton and Jack Watson both came in. I could see at once from their faces that all was well and my heart leapt to meet them.

'It's all right,' Bob said. 'All over. She's fine. She'll be all right. A very strange thing. Some scar tissue had tangled round her gall-bladder and completely strangled it. I took out her gall-bladder and her appendix too. You are very lucky to have been here for she was in a bad way.'

I wasn't allowed to see her all that day, and on the next I thought that she would never be done with sleeping, but the day after she was herself again and fretting to be out of the crowded little ward. On the fourth day after the operation Bob Peyton, wearing a natty white sports coat with a black pinstripe, thrown loosely over his shoulders, strode into the ward.

'I'll take the stitches out tomorrow,' he said to Beryl, 'and if you had a place to go to I'd let you go. This is costing you plenty, I know, but I can't have you climbing up on to that boat yet.'

'I have got a place to go to,' Beryl told him.

Everyone in the yacht harbour seemed to have heard of Beryl's operation, and had asked after her and offered help. Louise Meyer, until recently the captain and owner of the yacht *Porpoise*, which she had bought in America and sailed to New Zealand and back, had asked us to come and share her house on the north shore when Beryl came out of hospital.

'Well, then,' said Bob Peyton, 'let's have a look at those stitches. Perhaps I can take them out now, and let's see if we can get you out of the hospital by eleven because they won't let you out after that.'

By eleven the stitches were out and so was Beryl, and that afternoon Bob—our Bob—drove us over to the north shore in a borrowed car. On the way we ran into a rain squall and as we could not find the button to work the hood of the convertible, Beryl found herself once again exposed to driving rain. At Louise's home there was a comfortable bed, a hot bath whenever Beryl felt like one, and much kindness, but above all there was Beryl's indomitable will to speed her recovery. Within a week she had walked a mile to the store and we sailed exactly a month after her operation.

As we have voyaged round the world we have become deeply indebted to many people for their kindness, which it has been difficult or impossible to repay. Here in Hawaii our overdraft sank still further into the red, to Louise Meyer, Bob Peyton, Jack Watson, and to many others who stood by when Beryl was sick.

We sailed on June 5th, letting go our lines from where *Tzu Hang* was moored, with her bow almost on the Yacht Club lawn. Beryl was at the helm, suggesting in her old familiar way that I should have the engine ready to start in case of some shaming mishap, especially as the club verandah was full of people, having a drink before lunch, and ready to criticize any fault in seamanship.

We backed the jib and *Tzu Hang* slid out of her berth astern, then answered her helm obediently, swung her stern away and turned her bow to the channel. Bob and I set the main smartly. *Tzu Hang* soon gathered way, and as we hoisted the genoa and the water began to talk at her bow, she slid towards the mouth of the yacht harbour.

It was the start of the last leg of her journey and, in spite of Beryl's operation, not much later than we had intended to leave the islands, although we had had to forgo an intended visit to Kauai. Perhaps it would be the last long voyage that Beryl and I would sail in *Tzu Hang*, because we had other plans now. The trip round Cape Horn had been the climax of our cruising, and we were thinking of giving up the sea, at least in the way that we had known it. This had nothing to do with Beryl's operation, but rather that we were both growing older and felt that it was time we gave up the gypsy life to make a home. Whenever we talked about this Bob became reticent, as if he did not like to discuss it, or at least that he did not believe we were talking seriously.

It is impossible not to be sentimental about *Tzu Hang*, who has dominated our lives, as well as served us so well, for so long. We could not just put her up for sale and, since she is still fit for long passages, we could not keep her, looking more and more forlorn, while we became less and less inclined to take her on the voyages that she seems to love. We wanted not only a good home for her, but the right home for her, from where she might still be required to sail the seven seas.

It was good to be off. Bob and I, both worried about Beryl, were determined not to let her do too much. Beryl, still with a sore stomach, was prepared to let us 'hale and draw', as Drake insisted that his gentlemen should do, the same as the mariners, but for the rest she was equally determined to take her full share in running the ship. Fortunately, instead of pounding into the Trades, we had light weather and calm seas for the first three days, and on each day Beryl felt stronger.

It was not until the night of June 8th that we met the Trade Wind, so much in the north that we could only follow a course west of north. We hove to during the night, to ease the strain on Beryl's stomach, and because the course was not satisfactory, and if the truth be fully told, because we were all feeling a little sick. We had soup for dinner—a sign of the times.

On June 10th *Tzu Hang* was sailing well with the mizzen reefed, but still west of north and next day we were able to tack and sail a north-easterly course. Soon we were right in a 'high' again with light winds, grey days, mist, and everything dank below.

On our seventh day out we found a westerly wind which continued for three days, but on the eleventh day, with only 1,016 miles on the log, we were back in a 'high' again, the barometer reading 1023 mb and little or no wind. The usual course to sail from Hawaii is to sail due north, close-hauled into the Trades, until the westerlies are picked up. It is a rather longer route than the steamship route to Cape Flattery, but the way the weather was treating us, we might just as well have sailed a rhum line course. All the same it was treating us well, because light weather was easier on Beryl.

Now we had light south-easterly winds until June 22nd and on this day I reached an all-time low in Beryl's estimation. Before we left Victoria in 1955 she had had a stainless steel bucket made, into which the sink drained. John Guzzwell had fashioned a tilting box into which it fitted, beautifully made and dovetailed, like all John's work. The bucket could be tilted to receive rubbish other than that which came from the sink or for removal for emptying; a very practical affair, and because Beryl and John had designed it together, she loved it dearly. Every evening while we were at sea, she heaved it up on to the deck for the man on watch to empty or to empty herself. As it was heavy it was best to put a shoulder against the shroud, for both hands were required. One to hold the handle at the top, and one to hold a small handle at the side of the bottom for tipping.

On this evening Beryl handed the bucket to me, but just as I was going to empty it the ship gave an unexpected lurch and my shoulder slipped off the shroud. It was a case of saving the bucket or saving myself. I saved myself.

Bob heard us putting the ship about and came on deck to help, but just as we drew near again, the bucket, which had been floating well, surrendered to the sea and sank from sight. Bob looked at me appalled. The disaster was too dreadful for any comment, and Beryl went below without a word, leaving Bob and I looking at each other like two small boys in disgrace, although he had had no hand in it.

'But why didn't you go in after it?' she asked me later.

I thought that the idea of going in after a steel bucket, in oilskins, was rather far-fetched, until I arrived in Victoria and paid for a replacement.

On that day also, June 22nd, we saw a tropic bird, in 41° 28′N and 142° 14′W, far north for these birds in our experience.

At last, on Monday 23rd, we got a fair westerly wind, although the glass remained high, and made 141 miles by log. We had fork-tailed petrels flying about us and saw many murres, as well as the northern blackfooted albatross, or our old friend the mollyhawk. As we had done on the first time that we had sailed to Canada, we passed through thousands of small jellyfish, setting their little sails to the westerly wind. There were gale warnings out for the Straits of Juan de Fuca, and San Francisco had its record cold day for June of all time since recordings have been kept, 56° in San Francisco and 59° at Anchorage in Alaska.

On June 26th, while we still had a fresh westerly wind, a black and yellow tanker closed us, altered course to pass behind us, and then came past alongside. She was the *Atlantic Engineer* from Baltimore, on a northerly course. *Tzu Hang* was sailing well in a roughish sea, with main and mizzen reefed. She must have looked very small from the bridge of the tanker, whose captain now hailed us on the loud hailer.

'Are you all right?' he called.

In the cockpit of *Tzu Hang* we looked at each other in astonishment, then waved and shouted up towards the yellow painted bridge:

'We're O.K.'

'Do you wish me to report you?' The great voice thundered again, and our replies squawked back, a babble of small sea-birds:

'Thank you. To Victoria.'

He could not have heard a word, but satisfied now that we

were not in need of any assistance, the ship turned away and resumed its course to the northward, towards Anchorage and the warmer weather.

This day was crowded with shipping, for soon after the tanker's funnel had disappeared over the northern horizon our attention was attracted by a repeated white splash on the port bow, which turned out to be a grey whaler on the opposite course about two miles to the north. She turned down to intercept us, and soon we could make out a man in the barrel at the mast-head, a lively position, because with the sea now abeam, she was rolling violently. Shortly before the whaler crossed our bow she turned up towards us and slowed down, passing a cable away, then turned again, as handy as a polo pony, and came up on our quarter. She was burly and powerful, with a harpoon gun mounted on her high, flared bow. Several bulky figures ran along the deck to the bow as she closed us, and they, with the others looking out of the bridge windows and other points of vantage, all seemed to have cameras out.

'Look,' cried Beryl, 'they're wearing fur caps.'

'They're Russians,' shouted Bob. 'They've got the hammer and sickle on the funnel.'

If I had tried to draw a Russian ship for a child, I should have drawn it something like this, a workmanlike, rather shabby ship, with the Soviet badge on the funnel, and the crew all muffled up and wearing fur caps with loose ear flaps, but I should have left out the cameras. It was strange to see something so foreign almost in home waters.

'They seem to be awfully interested in us,' said Beryl, 'perhaps because were painted red.'

Presently, having waved and shouted at each other: 'Good voyage', from us in English, and presumably the same from them in Russian, and the camera fans on both sides being satisfied, the whaler spun round again, leaving a broad smooth slick as she turned, and continued on her original course.

For the next two days we made over 140 miles a day by log and picked up Cape Flattery radio beacon at midnight on June 28th. All along the line of the unseen coast to the north there was a loom of lights, not the lights themselves but a faint glow, as if at any moment lights might appear, and I guessed that it might be the lights of the salmon fishers. The wind had dropped, and *Tzu Hang* idled along as if her work was nearly done. There was a wonderful relaxed feeling, now that we had seen the loom of lights, of coming home at the end of a long passage.

Daylight came early, with Cape Flattery in sight, the wind right down and a long oily swell rolling in from the west. We hung on to our sail, sliding along with the swell helping us, past two big seiners working in the mouth of the Juan de Fuca Straits to the south of Vancouver Island. Finally we started the motor and headed for Port Renfrew on the northern side of the Straits, but just off the entrance a wind came again, so we changed our minds and sailed on up the coast for as long as daylight lasted. As we sailed, and sometimes motored, for the wind was fluky and we wanted to get as close to Victoria as possible, so that we could get in early next day, Beryl and I pointed out the well-known landmarks to Bob. We told him, with the excitement of coming home, of the other times that we had sailed up these Straits, and were anxious that he should enjoy the scenery.

As darkness fell we turned into a small indenture on the northern shore, with a few miles still to go, and anchored behind a rocky point. The water was still, reflecting the stars, and the tall firs stood motionless. There were no lights to be seen except those of a ship on her way down the Straits, no sound except the ripple of a fish moving and a small sound from the stony beach of 'the waters wappe and the waves wanne'. To all intents and purposes the voyage was over.

We talked in the cabin after supper of what we might do when we got in. Of hauling *Tzu Hang* out and painting her, of the new genoa that she needed, and a new mizzen, for we had had the old one for six years, and of whether she needed an overhaul for her engine.

'You know,' said Bob, 'if I can stand the winters, I wouldn't mind working here, if I could get a job.'

'You could get a job all right,' said Beryl, 'and you could live on *Tzu Hang* if you liked.'

'Yes. But what about all this rain I hear about. I don't like rain.'

'Heavens, Bob,' I said, 'anyone would think it doesn't rain in Melbourne or Wallaby Creek.'

'But I don't like it there either. Are you really going to sell *Tzu Hang*?'

Beryl and I looked at each other. 'Well—we think so,' I replied. 'After this another trip might be an anti-climax, and we're getting too involved in other things. We've got to do something about a home now.'

'If I could get a job and make enough money, I'd like to buy her,' he said.

We were staggered. We had never dreamed of it, and it was the best compliment that *Tzu Hang* has ever had, for by now he knew every bit of her, her good points and her bad. If he bought her she would go on sailing and we knew where she would go.

'Oh, Bob,' said Beryl with a catch in her voice. 'How wonderful. What could be nicer.'

'But it's still a big if,' he said, 'what with all this rain I hear about; and it might take some time.'

Three months later Beryl and I left *Tzu Hang* in order to return for a short time to England and Spain. *Tzu Hang* was moored in a private harbour on an island near Victoria, a harbour to which she came at the end of her first voyage from England, and to which she has often returned and always been welcomed. Bob was away working on a tugboat that tows a fuel barge to logging camps and depots far up the northern sounds. When he is not working he stays on *Tzu Hang*. Pwe stays on board or ashore as she wishes, but she appears to prefer the softer life in a house ashore.

When I left *Tzu Hang* I noticed that an otter had left its droppings on the edge of the float to which she is tied. While I waited at the dock by the motor boat that was to take us to the shore, a kingfisher was scolding from the top of one of the piles and a number of Canada geese flew, talking low, over the break-water, close past *Tzu Hang*, to the lake behind the house. These and the loons, murrelets and grebes will be her companions while we and Bob are away.

Presently I saw Beryl coming down towards me, with her slim figure and long mountaineer's stride, fully able again to 'hale and draw' with the mariners, and as the boat left the harbour, we both turned to look at *Tzu Hang*, as we always do whenever we leave her, no matter for how short a time. Her white masts had soon disappeared behind the trees on the point.

'Anyway,' said Beryl,' she'll be all right there—and with Bob.'

But when the wind blows and the rain lashes the window we think of her, and wonder whether we are glad—or not—that we, and Bob, are no longer still at sea.

Tzu Hang's voyages from Lymington to Victoria

From	Date	Arrived	Date	Days	Miles (Approx.)	Av. per day
Lymington	August 19th, 1968	Ria Arosa	August 25th, 1968	6	660	110
Ria Arosa	September 5th	Porto Praia	September 21st	16	1860	116·2
Porto Praia	September 24th	Montevideo	November 2nd	39	4340	111·3
Montevideo	November 27th	Talcahuano	January 2nd, 1969	36	3400	94·4
Talcahuano	January 20th, 1969	Juan Fernandez	January 23rd	3	360	120
Juan Fernandez	January 27th	San Felix	January 31st	4	420	105
San Felix	January 31st	Nuku Hiva	March 3rd	31	3600	116·1
Nuku Hiva	March 9th	Hilo	March 29th	15	1960	130·7
Hilo		Oahu				
Oahu	June 5th	Victoria	June 29th	24	2600	108·5
			Total	174	19200	110·4

Heavy Weather Sailing

Beryl disagrees with me when I say that we were lucky with the weather on our third attempt to sail round the Horn: 'We had regular Cape Horn weather,' she says. 'We were unlucky on the first two attempts.' That is true; but we knew that we might meet the same sort of weather again, and this time it would be head on.

If we had done so, we had the right ship, for I want no other in really heavy weather. She is as good as a lifeboat, but apart from her buoyancy, she is very strong, although not of exceptionally heavy construction. Her designer, H. S. Rouse, told me that when she was being unloaded on the dock in 1939, after being shipped from Hong Kong, she had slipped out of her slings on to the wharf, but that the only damage that she had sustained was a slight spreading of her lead keel. In the violent forces that she suffered in her two capsizes, apart from the loss of her masts, doghouse, and hatches in the first, and her masts in the second, there was no structural damage, except for the cracking of two deck beams.

I write of the management of a ship in heavy weather with hesitation, because my experience, although gained in many seas, is confined to one ship: a strong, deep-keeled, double-ended ketch, 46 foot long and of 11·8 foot beam, drawing 7 feet, with seven and a half tons of outside ballast. The best book that I have read on the subject is *Heavy Weather Sailing*, written by Adlard Coles, while the most succinct chapter that I have read on what to do in bad weather is written by Erroll Bruce in his book *Deep Sea Sailing*, headed 'Bad Weather'.

Tzu Hang has experienced gales in the North Sea, the Baltic, the Irish Sea, the Bering Sea, the Tasman Sea, the North Pacific, and the Southern Ocean. She has experienced violent winds of force 9 or more, but not of long duration, in a sumatra in the Malaccan Straits, in the Tsugaru-kaiko in Japan, and in the Mozambique Channel. The only times that she has been in danger and has had to fight for survival have been in the Southern Ocean.

It is difficult for even an experienced sailor to estimate the height of waves or to measure the strength of the wind accurately from the deck of a yacht. We have, now, on *Tzu Hang*, a small Swedish hand anemometer and when I have given wind strengths in this story they have been the mean of the readings taken from this instrument, usually held just above the doghouse hatch, with a third added to correct to the normal altitude at which reports are given. Otherwise we have been dependent on local weather reports. In the Baltic the nearest weather station reported the wind as blowing at 22 metres per second which put up a nasty short sea, and in the gale in the North Sea the local reports told of gales sweeping the whole of England, of ships sheltering behind Flamborough Head, of a Russian trawler wrecked in the Orkneys and of a Danish vessel sinking near the Dogger Bank. During all this *Tzu Hang* was hove to east of Holy Island. I find the hand anemometer a disappointing instrument, because it always seems to read rather lower than I am expecting. Perhaps it is inclined to read low as it is often sticky with salt water, but it is a fault on the right side, as we are all inclined to exaggerate when telling of weather conditions.

The highest readings that we recorded on this last trip were from 42 to 44 knots on the instrument itself. Unfortunately, we did not have it on our first two attempts to round Cape Horn nor have we ever had the synoptic charts that give such good support to the accounts of gales in *Heavy Weather Sailing*.

Every ship behaves in a different manner, and it is impossible to say: 'This is what you must do'. I can say only what I should do on my ship, but yours may need quite different treatment. It is also a mistake to claim that a yacht has come through worse gales and survived more dangerous seas than another, unless the writer also was in that other yacht. All descriptions of gales are dependent on the attitude of mind of the writer at the time, on his imagination, and on his power as a writer. At least *Tzu Hang*, after her two 'survival' gales, came back proudly carrying her scars of battle to show where she had been. I doubt whether any small yacht can survive a gale of force 10 or more, without showing some damage. However confident we may be that our ship will weather a gale of force 9, above that we are balanced precariously on the finger of fate.

So much has been written about Cape Horn and its horrors that it has developed a mystique all its own. If a sailor rounded it now without enormous seas and violent winds he would feel cheated, and, looking back, think: 'Surely the winds were stronger and the waves higher than I noted at the time.' It takes someone like Bill Tilman to take his yacht south of Cape Horn to Deception Island, and then to write: 'In my limited experience the sea here behaves very much as it does in other parts of the world. It is rough when the wind blows strongly and goes down when the wind drops.' The great waves that are reputed to roll unchecked round the bottom of the world, in fact probably do not roll much farther than the limit of the depressions that cause them. I have recently seen two weather charts each showing different depressions, each covering the whole of the North Atlantic, and each with a centre of 960 mb. Both of them were obviously capable of building up just as great waves as may be met with south and west of Cape Horn. No great ocean can claim to have the highest waves and the strongest winds but Cape Horn, even in summer, can claim to have a good percentage of them, and when I write of gales and what I should do to weather them, my thoughts turn to that part of the world, to waves 30 feet high, the wind force 9 or more, the spindrift blowing away over the sea, and the low clouds hurrying.

When, in spite of reduced sail, a ship going to windward is more under water than on top of it, when the strain from

pounding threatens that rigging will be carried away or plank-
ing damaged, when the going is too rough and uncomfortable
for the crew, then it is time to stop. Similarly, when running
downwind and the ship is threatening that she will soon take
charge, or running across the sea and it looks as if she may soon
be overwhelmed by a breaking crest, then it is time to do
something. A ship can lie a-hull, heave to, or run and reduce
her speed still further by taking down all sail and towing warps
aft. Whatever she does it is necessary that the captain should
know how she will behave under different circumstances, and
he must be prepared before the gale reaches its climax for the
action that he will take. Since I dislike lying a-hull most, I shall
deal with it first.

LYING A-HULL

'In a very violent storm we scudded before the wind and sea,
some time with only our bare poles, and the ship, by the mistake
of him that conn'd, broached to and lay in the trough of the
sea, which then went so high that every sea threatened to over-
whelm us, and indeed if any of them had broken on our deck,
it might have foundered us.' So wrote Captain John Cooke in
1683 in the *Revenge*, of a gale south of Staten Island, and it
reflects the opinion of most seamen, when a small ship, struggling
for survival, gets broadside on to the sea. In later days I believe
that it also reflects the opinion of such famous singlehanders as
Bill Nance and Robin Knox-Johnston. It is certainly the opinion
of Bill Nance's brother, Bob. Dampier was in the *Revenge* and
he and another seaman got her out of her unfortunate predicament by climbing up the foremast shrouds and spreading their
coats against them, so that the *Revenge* paid off, and was able to
survive the storm by running again before it.

When I read of the damage and the roll-overs recorded in
Adlard Coles' book, and remember other accounts of disaster,
all to do with ships that either by force of circumstances or by
choice were lying a-hull, I am convinced that in heavy seas it
is a most dangerous practice. Anyone, no matter what his
repute as a small boat sailor, who suggests that this is the way to

come through a 'survival' storm, bears a responsibility to future sailors that I am not prepared to share. I believe that almost every record of the loss of lifeboats, where the cause of the loss is known, will show that by some mischance they had become broadside on to the sea.

It is sometimes convenient to lie a-hull, as we did in the River Plate, but it should never be done in a severe gale, under dangerous wave conditions nor in a moderate gale when the current or tide produces the same effects. Erroll Bruce says, 'A wind force 12 would exert a thrust of some two tons on a typical 45-ft sloop and heel her far over to leeward; also, once the breaking tops of the waves are higher than a yacht's free-board it would be folly to offer the whole length of the ship to them, and the safest course in these conditions is to offer the bow or the stern.'

Adlard Coles quotes Nigel Warington Smyth in the *Royal Cruising Club Journal* of 1961, commenting on a roll-over suffered by the yacht *Tom Bowling*. '. . . a large breaking crest in a full gale may well be travelling at 15 to 20 knots, whereas the green water underneath it has virtually no horizontal motion. It follows that any vessel that is small enough or of shallow enough draft may be picked up and carried to leeward by the crest at great speed, until some part of her stabs down into the motion-less green water, and she will be smashed down, capsized, turned head over heels.' On a still smaller scale, anyone who has surfed in a dinghy on the front of a breaker knows what the inevitable end will be if he gets turned sideways.

When *Tzu Hang* was rolled over while lying a hull in 84° 30'S and 300 miles off the Chilean coast, the gale had been blowing for two whole days. I would estimate it now, with more knowledge than I had then, as blowing at force 10 and more from the west, with unlimited fetch. The waves must therefore have been at least 30 feet high.

Tzu Hang had been lying a-hull all the previous day, and during both days the crests were considerably higher than her freeboard. As a breaking wave approached we could hear it grumbling and growling from some distance away: the *tigres*, the Chilean sailors call them. Although we had had some nasty knocks, we had not been fairly hit by a big crest, but I knew that if one hit us as it broke, or soon after breaking, we would be in bad trouble. Soon after the glass had started to rise, and the wind had shifted to the south-west and was blowing even harder than before, we were hit by a wave that had already broken, and were rolled completely over. We lost our masts, the cockpit was burst open, and the doghouse was shifted to weather by the force with which she was driven into the sea.

I cannot understand now how I could have submitted to lying a-hull when I was aware of the danger, although perhaps not so aware of it as I am now. It must have been that we were both over-tired and therefore prepared to leave it to *Tzu Hang* to look after us and also that we were reluctant to give up our offing from the Chilean coast, and remembered how we had pitchpoled when running before a similar gale. A ship lying a-hull reminds me of a dog rolling over on its back before another and saying, 'Please do not bite me.' It is possible that by assuming this unhappy and passive position he may escape being bitten, but he will be badly hurt if he is. The same applies to a yacht lying a-hull, and the captain whose yacht comes through a severe gale intact by doing so, should show the same humble gratitude that the dog does when it escapes unhurt.

I have nothing against lying a-hull when the seas are not dangerous, but even then it is as well to know the speed of a yacht's drift. I allow two knots, but I have never known *Tzu Hang* drift faster than one and a half knots. When lying a-hull her helm is lashed down. She will then head up slightly towards the wind, fall off, and then gather way again. For the most part she is broadside to the sea and making about half a knot across the wind.

HEAVING TO

Rather than lying a-hull I would much prefer to heave to, provided that I could set some sail and the sail that I could set would stand up to the wind. I have been unable to find in

162

Adlard Coles' book any record of a yacht incurring damage while hove to.

When going to windward, before it is time to heave to, a yacht will already be down to its smallest headsail and deeply reefed main. It is therefore a simple business to put the ship on the other tack without touching the jib, or to winch the jib across and aback. If the speed of the boat is thereby reduced to perhaps half a knot, this is the most comfortable and safest way of riding out a storm.

Tzu Hang heaves to under her mainsail alone, reefed right down. It has then sufficient strength to keep her four to five points off the wind and just nosing into the sea. Her helm is lashed down and her way is insufficient to bring her head to wind. Perhaps it is the position of her mast or the high sheer of her bow that achieves this effect. With canvas dodgers firmly rigged on her quarter rails, her heading has improved. Her reefed mizzen, when set, brings her into the wind, but if she had roller-reefing on her mizzen we could set just sufficient sail to keep her pointing a little closer than she does without anything at all. When her reefed mizzen is set as well as the main or a small trysail, it is necessary to set her storm jib aback. She heaves to well like this, but loses more to leeward than she does with only the main set.

Our experience has been that when hove to the height of the waves has been insufficient to blank off the sails completely, so that she maintains her heading in the trough. Erroll Bruce quotes F. G. Martin as having recorded that he hove to safely in his 52 ft square-sterned *Chance* for 48 hours when the wind averaged 65 to 78 miles an hour. *Tzu Hang* has not hove to in gales of this force, nor do I know whether we could have done so in the two survival gales that we suffered. Perhaps we could have done if we could have set and reefed the main or a small trysail. But with a short-handed crew, setting and reefing the main and turning up into the wind, after running under storm jib or bare poles, could only be done with considerable danger, especially if it has been left until late. A small trysail could be set but that would need two people at the sail and one at the helm, unless the sail is already on the mast and ready for hoisting.

This is the key to success in a 'survival' storm. To decide what action may be necessary and to provide for it long before it is required, so that when the time arrives it can be put into effect quickly and safely. Bill Tilman, who took his yacht *Mischief* farther north and farther south than any of us and who must be the most experienced foul-weather sailor, prefers to heave to, rather than run in extreme conditions, particularly at night.

A Yorkshireman, Bill Crawley, the mate of a tanker, once helped us paint *Tzu Hang* while waiting for his ship in Durban. He had been at sea ever since he was a boy and as well as serving in the Merchant Service had sailed in trawlers north of the Arctic Circle and in an R.N. Survey ship in the Patagonian Channels. He had read *Once is Enough* and when he had got to know us better, told us in his direct Yorkshire way: 'You did wrong, you know.'

'Why wrong?'

'Well,' he said, 'you should have faced up into it.'

They say that when the Angles settled in England, the acute Angles went south, the obtuse Angles to Scotland, but the right Angles came to Yorkshire. Bill Crawley was one of the right Angles, and his advice is worth listening to.

RUNNING

There are three good reasons for running before a gale: first, if the wind is blowing the way that you are going, secondly, if sail or rigging has carried away so that it is forced upon you, and thirdly if the wind is so violent that sail cannot be carried. While running before a gale a ship may be exposed to three dangers. She may be pooped, she may run so fast that she starts surfing, or gets out of control and threatens to broach to, or she may be pitchpoled stern over bow.

Pooping is due to the stern not lifting in time to a wave, or to the shape of a wave which curls over and breaks just as it reaches the stern. Most yachts, running before a full gale, are boarded sooner or later and the force of the water battering the helmsman is always surprising. He may easily be washed out of the cockpit if he is not tied in. For most well-designed yachts there is no particular danger in this. They shake themselves like a labrador coming out of a pond, running on to the slop of water in the cockpit and the gurgling of the cockpit drains as if nothing had happened. For a yacht with a large open cockpit, or one that opens directly into the saloon without a bridge deck, it is a much more important and dangerous affair.

A wave that curls over and breaks on the after part of the ship is more dangerous and can do considerable damage. *Carronade*, the 31-foot Australian sloop sailed by Andy Wall, was boarded by a heavy sea that smashed the cover of the after-hatch and sent a large amount of water below. Pooping is probably dependent on the speed at which a yacht is running, and to the disturbance that she is making in the water. Its likelihood may be lessened by altering the speed of the ship to suit the conditions and the timing of the waves. In order to avoid further pooping she should run either a little faster or a little slower, depending on the speed with which she was running at the time of her first pooping. *Tzu Hang* has a buoyant stern, makes hardly any disturbance and is very rarely pooped. On each occasion I think it occurred because she was running too slowly for an impatient sea.

RUNNING TOO FAST

When a ship is running too fast, she answers less readily to the helm, taking the bit between her teeth, and swinging one way or the other, so that the helmsman has to be continually on the alert to anticipate and check her movements, and to prevent her swinging right round and broaching to. *Carronade*, with her fast and easily driven hull, on more than one occasion got above herself and threatened to take charge on her way to the Horn. Her crew brought her under control immediately by towing warps with motor car tyres attached. Bob said that the result was just as if a runaway horse had suddenly answered quietly to the bit, and is convinced that when the time comes to take speed off a ship in this manner, her stern should be presented directly to the waves.

This, although in accordance with long-established practice, is contrary to the solution offered by Bernard Moitessier. Once, when in a dangerous gale, he towed warps and a loading net, keeping his stern to the sea, he got into such a position that he was convinced he was about to be pitchpole. He dramatically cut away his warps, and ran at between five and seven knots, with his stern at an angle of 15° to 20° to the sea. From then on he considered that he was never again in such acute danger.

As I understand his account, in spite of the warps that he was towing, he got into a 'surfing position' with his stern up and the whole of the front of his boat buried in the water. This is a very alarming position to be in and there is no wonder that he expected *Joshua* to pitchpole. She must have been within a fraction of doing so. Moitessier concludes that this was the position that *Tzu Hang* got into and which caused her to pitch-pole. In fact it was not.

Tzu Hang was running before a gale which I should estimate now to have been force 10 or more. At no time was she running too fast, nor was she particularly difficult to steer, and the warps that she was trailing seemed to have no effect one way or the other as they were often carried up in the breaking crests. She was not surfing nor ever attempted to surf. When she does, after a preliminary surge as her stern lifts, her bow comes up and she rushes along with the after part of her deck covered with breaking water, running on each side of the cockpit coaming. She will only get into this position if she is running at about 7 or 8 knots, which she certainly was not doing at the time. The most striking part of this alarming event is the high angle of her bow, and the jets of water that she throws up on each side of it like a fast motor boat. I have only seen her do this once but we have felt her do it, when she has been running under twins and we have been below. While she is surfing there is no control at all, but she has always run straight until the wave left her.

When she pitchpoled a very high and exceptionally steep

wave hit her, considerably higher than she was long. It must have broken as she assumed an almost vertical position on its face. The movement was extremely violent and quick. There was no sensation of being in a dangerous position with disaster threatening. Disaster was suddenly there. Whether she had been 20° to it or her stern directly presented to it, or whether she had been running at 2 or 7 knots could, in this case, have made no difference. Her stern came up and just went on going with no hesitation at all right over the bow.

When Bernard Moitessier, that fine seaman, offers an opinion, it should be well considered, because he has twice sailed *Joshua* round Cape Horn from the Atlantic to the Pacific, but his answer is not necessarily the right one for all yachts, any more than mine is, and it requires a superman to steer accurately like this through a dark night. In my opinion it would be far safer to run directly in front of the sea. Even if his theory is correct for other yachts, tired men and irregular waves are apt to defy it.

A few years ago *Tzu Hang* was running from Reykjavik to the north-west point of Iceland in a south-west gale. It was a dark night and the wind force 9 with a heavy sea on her quarter. *Tzu Hang* had only her storm headsail set, and in order to prevent it jibing over and back again, with sudden strains on sheet, halyard, and stay, we were running with the wind on our quarter, which gave us a nice offing from the inhospitable shore. *Tzu Hang* was tearing along through the night in the conditions that she seems to like best, and I was happy and singing at the tiller, since we were going fast in the direction that we wished to go.

Suddenly I felt, rather than saw, a monster wave breathing down my neck and coming at a slightly different angle. The next moment we were hit with a shock that felt as if a ten-ton lorry had run into us. *Tzu Hang* was knocked bodily sideways and the tiller was wrenched out of my hand and thumped against the leeward coaming at the limit of its travel. I found myself standing vertically on the lee side of the cockpit, like a jockey whose horse has pecked at Becher's Brook. *Tzu Hang's* masts went down to the horizontal, but she came up again and ran on straight and true, to the sound of startled queries from below. A lesser boat would have broached and probably rolled over. I thought of bigger waves in the Southern Ocean and wondered what would have happened if she had been hit by one of them. However, keeping the stern at a slight angle to the sea may prevent a boat from surfing if she is showing that inclination.

OIL

Oil is something that all boats should carry and very rarely do. I had intended never to go South again without a large oil tank with through hull fittings and easily operated cocks. Then, in a storm, I could leave a long and ever-widening path of oil behind me. We did not fit an oil tank before going South because of the expense, because an adequate supply would take up a lot of space and because we did not anticipate running before a gale, if it could be possibly avoided, since we were going in the other direction.

SEA ANCHOR

I have no great faith in a sea anchor streamed from the bow for a yacht of *Tzu Hang*'s size, as she will drag it round until she lies broadside to the seas. Streamed from the stern it should do very well for *Tzu Hang* since she is a double-ender with a buoyant stern, a small cockpit, and a strong doghouse. We didn't carry one because they take up a great deal of room. When running, motor tyres should be almost as efficient, will put less strain on the hawsers, and can be used as fenders in an emerency.

RUNNING WITH A SINGLE HEADSAIL

Robin Knox-Johnston ran with a single headsail braced amid ships. I should have thought that the disadvantage in doing this is that the sail jibes backwards and forwards however strongly it is sheeted home. *Tzu Hang* ran many miles in the Southern Ocean with a single headsail sheeted in on the port tack. She had no rudder but kept the seas on her quarter. However, under

normal conditions we prefer to steer and keep the sail full by
sailing a few degrees off the wind.

'TZU HANG' IN A SURVIVAL STORM

In the end, in a battle for survival, there is no final answer, and
no one can be assured that a small yacht will see it through. It
depends whether or not she is hit by some particular wave,
towering and breaking at just the wrong time. As far as *Tzu
Hang* is concerned, if caught out in a severe gale, I should follow
the old and tried practices of the sea. If possible I would ride
out the gale by heaving to. If it was impossible to set or carry
sail I would turn and run. If my ship threatened to get out of
control by surfing or broaching I would tow warps astern to
which were attached some form of sea anchor. I would avoid,
at all costs, lying broadside to the sea.

I hope that *Tzu Hang* will meet many more gales and will
bear them as she has borne others before, but I hope that she
will never again meet such a storm as those that turned her
over, when alone, battered and dwarfed by the seas, she
endured and survived to save herself and her crew.